Getting Your Child to Say "Yes" to School

Getting Your Child

■ *Christopher A. Kearney* ■   *A Guide for*

to Say "Yes" to School

Parents of Youth With School Refusal Behavior

OXFORD
UNIVERSITY PRESS

2007

OXFORD

UNIVERSITY PRESS

Oxford University Press, Inc., publishes works that further
Oxford University's objective of excellence
in research, scholarship, and education.

Oxford   New York
Auckland   Cape Town   Dar es Salaam   Hong Kong   Karachi
Kuala Lumpur   Madrid   Melbourne   Mexico City   Nairobi
New Delhi   Shanghai   Taipei   Toronto

With offices in
Argentina   Austria   Brazil   Chile   Czech Republic   France   Greece
Guatemala   Hungary   Italy   Japan   Poland   Portugal   Singapore
South Korea   Switzerland   Thailand   Turkey   Ukraine   Vietnam

Copyright © 2007 by Oxford University Press, Inc.

Published by Oxford University Press, Inc.
198 Madison Avenue, New York, New York 10016

www.oup.com

Oxford is a registered trademark of Oxford University Press

Cataloging-in-Publication Data is available from the Library of Congress.
ISBN 978-0-19-530630-9 (pbk.)

Contents

Getting Your Child to Say "Yes" to School

What Is School Refusal Behavior?

"Jonathan has missed the last week of school! I can't seem to get him out of bed in the morning. I feel so frustrated. What can I do?"

"Ashlee has a lot of trouble going to school in the morning. She cries a lot and just seems so unhappy. This is so stressful for all of us. How can we help our daughter?"

"I just found out that Reggie has been skipping some classes at school. I can't believe it! Why is he doing this? What happens now?"

"Will just seems to mope around, especially on Sunday nights. He's always asking us to put him in home schooling. I'm so confused. Should I teach him at home?"

"I can get Madison to go to school, but only after a long, drawn-out fight every morning! I'm so tired of this. What can we do to make the morning easier?"

"Gisela cries all the time at school and always wants me there. She hangs on to me at the playground as I try to drop her off. I feel so bad for her. Should I just miss a few days of work and go to class with her?"

"Brett always seems to have stomachaches and headaches in the morning before school. He says he can't go. Should I make him go? What's wrong?"

Do any of these situations sound familiar to you? When a child has trouble attending school, or seems so unhappy about going to school, family members are often frustrated, distressed, shocked, confused, and angry. But that's understandable. We naturally expect our children to eat their food, play with friends, sleep at night—and go to school in the morning! If a child has trouble doing any of these things, then family tension builds, everyone fights, and you may start wondering: What do we do now? What is going to happen? How can I get my child back to school? All of these reactions are perfectly normal.

Having a child with trouble attending school is so upsetting because we do not like for our kids to be distressed and we worry what will happen if they don't receive their education. And, let's face it, we have to get to work in the morning! I have two young children of my own; I know the rush in the morning and what can happen if one of them does not want to leave the house. What makes trouble attending school even more upsetting is that the problem can be hard to understand and resolve. But be assured: you *can* get your child to school with less distress! The main purpose of this book is to cover the different aspects of this problem and give you the means to handle all kinds of "school refusal behavior."

School Refusal Behavior: What Is That?

School refusal behavior refers to a child's difficulty attending school or remaining in classes for an entire day. You may hear people use other terms such as truancy or school phobia when discussing attendance problems, but these terms are not very helpful. For example, "truancy" usually refers to youths who miss school without their parents' knowledge. If you are reading this book, however, you likely know about your child's attendance problems. In addition, "school phobia" usually refers to kids who are afraid of something specific at school, but this is rare. I like the term "school refusal behavior" because it includes *all* children who have trouble going to or being in school. In other words, your child's situation should be in this book! So, for our discussion, let's stick to "school refusal behavior."

School refusal behavior means that a child may actually have *different kinds* of attendance problems. A brief look at these problems is shown in

Figure 1.1
Forms of school refusal behavior

School attendance with stress and pleas for nonattendance	Repeated misbehaviors in the morning to avoid school	Repeated tardiness in the morning followed by attendance	Periodic absences or skipping of classes	Repeated absences or skipping of classes mixed with attendance	Complete absence from school during a certain period of time	Complete absence from school for an extended period of time
X	X	X	X	X	X	X

figure 1.1. A longer look at these problems follows here. Think about the problems that seem to apply most to your child and place a checkmark next to those that do:

- Margaret does in fact go to school but is often stressed while there and cries or has stomachaches or headaches when near school. She always seems to be pestering her mom and dad to stay home and constantly asks to be enrolled in home schooling. Margaret also clings to her parents in the morning as they try to get her into the school building.

- Hunter hopes to miss school that day by misbehaving in the morning: his common behaviors include dawdling, refusing to move, locking himself in a room or car, and throwing temper tantrums. Hunter's parents often get their son to school but only after a huge battle between 6 a.m. and 9 a.m.

- Stacy is often late to school as a result of dawdling or the other misbehaviors just mentioned for Hunter. She often shows up to school during a second-period class or at 10:30 that morning. Sometimes she is very anxious in the morning as well.

- Parker will attend school only if one of his parents stays with him at school.

- Jackson skips one or more classes during the day, such as ditching school after lunch to be with friends or missing a class that requires a test or oral presentation that day. He also has trouble eating in the school cafeteria with others.

- Melissa misses a complete school day every so often, such as once or twice per week.

- Garrett has a history of missing long stretches of school days, such as a couple of weeks or even an entire semester.

Which of these situations sounds most familiar to you? Does your child have an attendance problem that is different from the ones listed here? If so, please describe it by writing in this space (and e-mail it to me when you get a chance!—my address is chris.kearney@unlv.edu):

_____

_____

_____

_____

Did you place several checkmarks next to the attendance problems I listed? If you did, that's okay. Many children with trouble attending school show different kinds of attendance problems over time. Consider, for example, the case of Justin:

Justin is a 12-year-old boy who has just entered middle school and is having some problems adjusting to the new setting. He seems a bit overwhelmed by the fact that he suddenly has several new teachers and classes and much more homework than before. In addition, Justin is nervous about so many of the older kids at his school and whether he will miss the bus after school. Lately he has been having problems getting up in the morning. During the past week alone, Justin threw a temper tantrum on Monday in an attempt to miss school, skipped a class at school on Tuesday, was completely absent from school on Wednesday, was late to school on Thursday, and had no trouble attending school on Friday!

Obviously, a situation like Justin's can be pretty frustrating for everyone involved. One of the main problems of school refusal behavior is its *unpredictability*: a parent is often unsure what kind of problems to expect on any given morning. This is why a key goal of this book is to cover *all* of the attendance problems you are likely to see in the morning and during the school day and to help you address each of these. Let's talk some more about what this book is about.

What Is This Book About?

The main purpose of this book is to help parents and kids find solutions to the problem of school refusal behavior. In doing so, I am relying on my many years of experience working with these groups and helping parents get their kids back to school. As such, I can provide *very specific suggestions* for what you can do in the morning and the rest of the day to ensure that your child goes to school and stays in school for the entire day. In addition, I can provide you with some ways of helping your child go to school with less distress.

Chapter 1 is devoted to helping you understand what school refusal behavior is, as well as some of the common problems that come with this behavior. Chapter 2 is designed to help you understand and determine the main reasons why your particular child is having trouble going to school. Discovering why your child is refusing school is very important because methods of getting one child back to school are not necessarily best for getting another child back to school. For example, we have to treat 6-year-old Jabari, who is crying to be with his mom, differently from 15-year-old Samantha, who is ditching school after lunch and does not want her parents to know where she is. One size does not fit all when it comes to kids with school refusal behavior!

Once we know why your child is refusing school, we can then discuss specific methods to help him or her go to school with less distress. These specific methods will be covered in chapters 3, 4, 5, and 6. Although chapters 3 through 6 are designed for different kinds of school refusal behavior, I recommend that you read each chapter. You might find, for example, a certain suggestion that applies particularly well to your situation. Finally, in chapter 7, I focus on ways of trying to prevent school refusal behavior from happening again and provide some sources for more detailed information if you are interested. However, everything you need to know to get a child back to school with less distress is in this book.

Will This Book Help Me?

This book will be more helpful for certain families than others (table 1.1). Let's explore different topics to help you decide whether this book is right for you.

Table 1.1

Will This Book Be Helpful to You?

This book will be more helpful to you if:	This book will be less helpful to you if:
Your child is having trouble going to school or staying in school for an entire day.	Your child goes to school with ease and stays there but has trouble completing homework or listening at home.
Your child has recently started refusing to go to school.	Your child has been refusing school for a long period of time.
Your child has relatively few symptoms or problems.	Your child has many symptoms or problems.
Your child does not have severe behavior problems.	Your child has severe behavior problems such as attention-deficit/ hyperactivity disorder, aggression, delinquent behavior, substance abuse, extreme anxiety and/or depression, and bipolar disorder.
Your child should be going to school but is not.	Your child is having trouble going to school because of some legitimate problem such as illness or actual school threat.
Your child's school refusal behavior is fairly stable.	Your child's school refusal behavior is getting much worse by the day.
You are sure you want your child to go to school.	You are not sure you want your child to go to school.

Actual School Attendance Problems

This book will be helpful if your child is actually having trouble going to school or staying in school for an entire day. Many parents ask me about their child's refusal to complete homework, inability to make friends or speak at school, and trouble reading. These are important issues that can occur *with* school refusal behavior, but they will not be specifically addressed in this book. Instead, I focus mostly on attendance and distress issues. If you feel that issues other than school refusal behavior apply to your child, then you may wish to consult a qualified mental health professional.

Length of School Attendance Problems

This book will be helpful if your child has recently been having trouble going to school for *less than 2 months*. However, the book may also be helpful to some parents whose child previously had problems attending school. For example, this book might be helpful for someone like Claire:

Claire is a 14-year-old girl in ninth grade who is having great difficulty attending school this September. Her parents say that Claire often feels bad when attending school and has already started ditching some classes to be with her friends. Claire had similar problems last year, but her attendance improved after a couple of months and she had no problems going to school from November to June.

If your child has been having constant problems attending school for more than 4 months, then you may wish to consult a qualified mental health professional.

Other Problems

This book is intended for children and families who have fewer and less severe problems. For example, the book will be more useful if your child's school refusal behavior is his or her *main and sole behavior problem*. If your child is refusing school *and* has other problems such as general noncompliance (not listening) at home or lack of friends, or more severe behavior problems like attention-deficit/hyperactivity disorder (ADHD) or extreme depression, then you may wish to consult a qualified mental health professional. In addition, this book will be more helpful if your family members get along fairly well. You may be "up in arms" about your child's trouble attending school, but this is normal. However, to get a child to go to school with less distress, *parents must develop a united front that includes mutual support*. If you and your spouse or partner seem to be arguing or fighting a lot about many things, or if either of you has significant anxiety, depression, substance use, or other problems, you may wish to consult a qualified mental health professional.

Refusing School for Legitimate Reasons

This book will be more helpful if your child *should* be going to school but is still having trouble doing so. The book will be less helpful if your child is having trouble attending school for some *legitimate reason*. Legitimate reasons for not attending school include:

- True medical illness such as asthma

- Medical doctor, dentist, optometrist, or other professional appointment

- Family emergencies and ceremonies such as funerals

- Religious holidays

- Haphazard weather conditions

- School-sanctioned release time for work-study, college, or other educational programs

- Homelessness or other severe family conditions that prevent school attendance

- True school-based threats to personal self or property

True school-based threats usually include *excessive teasing, taunting, bullying, verbal or physical assaults or intimidation, theft, property damage, and sexual or other maltreatment from peers, school officials, or others.* If a child is refusing school because he or she does not want to face these threats, then the threats must be resolved *before* any of the methods in this book are tried.

In this case, I recommend that parents, school officials, and perhaps legal officials meet to resolve the threat. Solutions may include removing the bully or threat from school and reducing social isolation of the victim. In particular, every instance of bullying must be reported and dealt with swiftly. Children are encouraged to travel the school with friends, and school officials are encouraged to better monitor potential threats and actively work to prevent them. If a bullying or otherwise threatening situation is resolved and a child is *still* having trouble going to school, then the strategies described in this book can be employed.

In related fashion, some children have trouble attending school because of a *poor school climate.* In particular, youths may complain of tedious curricula, unnecessary homework, "dinosaur-age" teachers who make class boring, and mean-spirited educators. Other youths lament being in a racial minority at school, feeling generally threatened by their peers, being ignored by teachers, suffering the problems of overcrowded classrooms, and having to adhere to endless school regulations that make little sense. Some children adjust to these situations by entertaining themselves in school, but other children actively refuse to go to school.

In some cases, a child's complaints about school are understandable and should be addressed. In this situation, I recommend having extended and detailed discussions with school officials (guidance counselors, teachers, others) to see what daily changes can be made to enhance a child's satisfaction at school (within reason, of course). Options may include changing class schedules and teachers and curricula (if possible and appropriate), integrating a child into extracurricular activities, and establishing extra tutoring services. Sometimes the use of 504 and individualized education plans are helpful in these situations if they apply. These plans allow for changes in regular school practices to fit the needs of a particular child who has problems that interfere with his or her ability to learn.

Parents sometimes consider switching schools for their children. Often, however, such consideration comes only after persistent child demands or requests to go to a new school. *In general, I strongly recommend that you try to resolve your child's attendance issues within your child's current school.* Allowing a child to switch schools is not always the best option because many of the problems at the old school, such as feeling socially isolated, will be present at the new school as well. Switching schools should be considered only as a last resort unless the child's current school climate is extremely threatening, hostile, or unbearable.

School Withdrawal by Parents

Some parents deliberately keep their children home from school, a situation known as *school withdrawal*. In addition, other parents are not particularly concerned about their children's school attendance. Obviously, this book would not be very helpful in these situations. I am assuming you are reading this book because you *do* want your child to go to school with less distress and that you *are* highly motivated to help him or her do so.

Why do some parents deliberately keep their children home from school? Common reasons include:

- Babysitting younger brothers and sisters

- Asking an adolescent to secure a job to help support the family

- Hiding marks from child abuse from school officials

- Protecting children from kidnapping by an ex-spouse

- Helping parents with daily chores

- Punishing the child for some misbehavior

- Trouble on the part of parents to separate from their child

- Excessive conflict with school officials

- Pursuing unnecessary home schooling

- Keeping the child at home as a "safety person" if a parent is highly anxious

- Fear of harm directed toward the child at school

What Problems Come With School Refusal Behavior?

What are the common behavior problems found in children with trouble attending school? As you may already know, children with trouble attending school are likely to show different kinds of behavior problems. Often these behavior problems can be divided into those that are *less obvious or clear* and those that are *more obvious or clear*. When a child is having trouble attending school, he may have some of the following *less obvious* problems:

- General/nonspecific anxiety or apprehension or worry that something bad will happen

- Nervousness about being around others or having to perform before others

- General sadness or moping about having to go to school

(NOTE: Often a child's anxiety and sadness occur together and it is hard to tell which is which; the child may instead appear cranky, report a sense of dread or "feeling bad" about school, and wish to be left alone. This is common in children with attendance problems, and I will talk more about this kind of nervous/sad behavior in chapter 2.)

- Irritability and restlessness

- Fear of something specific to school, such as a school bus, cafeteria, or teacher

- Physical problems such as stomachaches, headaches, abdominal pain, trembling, nausea, vomiting, frequent urination, muscle tension, diarrhea, dizziness, or fainting. Other physical problems might include heart tremors (palpitations), lightheadedness, shortness of breath, hyperventilation, sweating, and menstrual symptoms.

- Trouble sleeping or a feeling of being overly tired, especially in the morning

- Trouble concentrating

- Withdrawal from others

In addition, a child with trouble attending school may show problems that are *more obvious*, such as the following:

- Temper tantrums, including crying, screaming, kicking, and flailing arms and legs

- Tearfulness or sobbing

- Refusal to get out of bed or even move in the morning

- Noncompliance or defiance to parent or teacher commands, which means failing to do as told or outright refusing to do as told

- Locking oneself in a room or car to avoid school

- Running away from home to avoid school or running away from the school building

- Clinging to an adult, especially Mom or Dad

- Lying

- Asking the same or similar questions over and over, such as "Do I really have to go to school tomorrow?," "Can't I just stay home?," or "What if something bad happens?" These questions may come with statements said over and over, such as "I hate school," "I don't want to go to school," or "You can't make me go to school."

- Verbal or physical aggression toward oneself or others to miss school

Do any of these behaviors look familiar to you? Please review the lists again and place a checkmark next to those that seem to apply most to your child. Does your child show certain behaviors not listed here? If so, please describe them by writing in this space (and e-mail it to me when you get a chance!—my address is chris.kearney@unlv.edu):

_____

_____

_____

_____

If you made several checkmarks next to the behaviors listed above, that's okay. In fact, that is what I would expect! Indeed, many children with trouble attending school show many of these behaviors, and these behaviors can even change from day to day! Consider, for example, the case of Lindsey:

Lindsey is an 8-year-old girl who has enormous problems getting to school in the morning. Her parents say that Lindsey will not get out of bed until the very last minute and dawdles through her morning tasks until everyone is late getting out of the house. Although this has led to a lot of family fights, Lindsey says she does not want to go to school because she feels "nervous" and "crummy" in the morning and "awful" while at school. When asked why she feels this way, though, Lindsey cannot say. In addition, Lindsey has been known to throw temper tantrums in the morning, cry in the car on the way to school, and even call her mother names for trying to make her go to school.

You can see in Lindsey's case that she has problems that are *less obvious or clear* (feeling nervous, crummy, and awful) and problems that are *more obvious or clear* (dawdling, tantrums, name calling). Most children with trouble attending school show less obvious *and* more obvious behavior problems. In addition, as mentioned earlier, these problems often change from day to day or week to week.

If your child is having trouble attending school and you seem overwhelmed by all of his or her different behaviors, this is completely normal. I see this all the time. We'll work on these behaviors together and I will show you in chapter 2 how to view your child's behavior in a simpler and easier way. Before we do that, though, let's talk some more about what school refusal behavior is.

How Common Is School Refusal Behavior? Am I the Only One?

Please believe me: your child is not the only one having trouble going to school. For many years, I have directed a treatment clinic for children with school refusal behavior and anxiety disorders, and I can't tell you the number of times that parents have expressed surprise that such a clinic exists or needs to exist! In other words, they have trouble believing that problems attending school can be so common. But these problems are actually very common.

Up to 28% of children and adolescents will, at some time during their young lives, have trouble attending school. This figure includes all of the different forms of school refusal behavior mentioned earlier, such as distress during school, morning misbehaviors, tardiness, skipping classes, and full-day absences. This means that trouble attending school is even more common than many childhood problems that you may have heard of, such as attention-deficit/hyperactivity disorder or depression.

What Do Children With School Refusal Behavior Look Like?

Well, they look like little people. I am joking, of course, but in fact it is hard to tell exactly what kind of child is most likely to have problems attending school. For example, school refusal behavior seems to occur in boys and girls equally and does not seem more common to any particular racial or ethnic group (though school dropout rates do differ by ethnicity).

In addition, children from many different countries have trouble going to school.

Although gender, ethnicity, and geography seem largely unrelated to school refusal behavior, age is a different story. The most common age for a child to have trouble attending school is 10 to 13 years. This fact surprises some people, who may have thought that school refusal behavior was most common in very young children. Instead, youths who are entering adolescence and middle school seem to be at particular risk.

Children who are entering a new school building for the first time also seem to be at risk of having problems attending school. This includes children entering kindergarten or first grade, middle school, and high school, but can also include children who recently moved from one area to another and who have to enroll in a new school district. Many younger children also have trouble going to school for a full day for the first time.

Keep in mind, however, that any school-aged child, such as one in fifth grade who has been going to the same elementary school for years, can have attendance problems. In many of these cases, problems attending school grow more and more intense over the years. Consider, for example, the case of Matt:

Matt is a 10-year-old boy in fifth grade who has missed the past 2 weeks of school. His parents report that Matt's problems attending school actually started in second grade, when he cried during much of September, but seemed to improve afterward. In third grade, Matt's nervousness and anxiety about school lasted until the latter part of October. In fourth grade, Matt began missing some school days altogether because he often seemed sick. Most of these days missed were Mondays. Toward the end of fourth grade, Matt made such a fuss about going to school that he missed the entire last week of school. His parents thought that fifth grade might be different, but Matt immediately started refusing to leave home for school as soon as the school year started.

If your child has been developing greater and greater problems attending school over the years, be assured that this is common. What is most important, however, is to nip the problem in the bud before the absenteeism becomes severe.

How Can I Help My Child Adjust to a New School or Her First Time at School?

Adjusting to new things can be hard for all of us, and children sometimes have special problems adjusting to a new school building or starting school for the first time. What can you do to help your child during this tough transition? Some suggestions follow. These suggestions may also be helpful if your child has previously had problems attending school and you are worried that the problems may recur at the start of the school year:

- Attend all orientation sessions that are held at your child's school before the start of the school year. Be sure to bring your child with you!

- Purchase or secure all necessary school supplies at least 1 week before the start of school.

- With your child, walk around the school so that you and he become *very familiar* with the layout of the school. In particular, show your child his classroom(s) as well as the school cafeteria, gymnasium, library, art and music centers, playground, and other relevant areas. Ask your child if she has any questions about getting from one place in school to another, and address any concerns she has.

- Arrange for you and your child to meet your child's school guidance counselor and teacher(s). Show your child the location of the main office and the guidance counselor's office so that he or she can stop by during the day to ask questions or express concerns.

- Talk to your child about the school bus, including bus number, stops, times, and what to do if he or she misses the school bus. Practice the routine of getting to the school bus stop near home in the morning and at school in the afternoon.

- About 2 weeks before the start of school, have your child begin the morning routine as if preparing for school (weekdays only). In other words, he or she should arise from bed at a certain early time, wash, eat, dress, brush teeth, and complete other regular morning activities as if he or she were going to school that day. That way, going to school the first day will not be made more difficult because of unfamiliarity with the morning routine.

- The night before school starts, have a relaxed conversation with your child about any last-minute concerns he or she might have about going to school the next day.

- Plan to make your schedule flexible during your child's first day of school in case he or she is jittery or takes a while to enter the school building. In a neutral and firm but supportive manner, require your child to go to school.

Medical Conditions

As mentioned earlier, many children who refuse to attend school have physical complaints such as headaches and stomachaches. However, other medical conditions may also be present. For example, asthma and other respiratory illnesses are a leading cause of absenteeism worldwide. Sleep problems are also frequent. Other common medical problems include influenza, allergies, dysmenorrhea (pain or discomfort surrounding a menstrual period), diabetes, head lice, and dental disease. School refusal behavior has also been linked to chronic conditions such as:

- *Cancer* (uncontrolled growth of abnormal cells)

- *Chronic fatigue syndrome* (a general condition involving unexplained fatigue, weakness, muscle pain, and trouble thinking)

- *Crohn's disease* (an inflammatory problem often affecting the small intestine and colon)

- *Dyspepsia* (upset stomach or indigestion)

- *Hemophilia* (a bleeding disorder from poor clotting)

- *Irritable bowel syndrome* (changes in bowel habits involving diarrhea, constipation, abdominal pain, and cramping)

Of course, any other medical condition not listed here could also affect a child's school attendance. If your child has any physical complaints or medical conditions related to school attendance problems, then be sure to first pursue comprehensive medical examinations and treatment. True medical problems must be addressed *before* using any procedures in this book. Do not assume that your child is faking physical symptoms. I once treated a 9-year-old girl who complained of stomach pain when attending school. Everyone thought she was making this up, but she was eventually diagnosed with a stomach ulcer!

> *If your child has any physical complaints or medical conditions related to school attendance problems, then be sure to first pursue comprehensive medical examinations and treatment.*

A good place to start in this situation is with your family medical doctor or neighborhood children's clinic. Be sure to fully describe your child's symptoms and when they occur. Keep a log of your child's symptoms so you know when they occur and how long they last. Note especially any symptoms that "magically" disappear on Saturdays and Sundays. If your doctor rules out any medical cause for any physical symptoms your child may have, then the procedures in this book may be more helpful.

That said, some children fake physical symptoms to try to get out of having to go to school. Sickness is a legitimate excuse for getting us out of many obligations, and children learn this at an early age. In addition, some children have minor physical symptoms that are not severe enough to show up on any medical test. These minor symptoms, such as stomach distress, are real, but some children make them seem worse for attention or to try to stay out of school. I will talk about how to address these situations in chapter 5.

What Happens to Children Who Refuse School for a Long Time?

Okay, time for some bad news. As you may already know, a child who is having trouble attending school for a long period of time may be at risk for certain kinds of related problems. In the short run, these children can become quite distressed. In addition, as a child misses more and more school, grades decline, schoolwork piles up, and friendships become strained or broken. Getting a child to go back to school after several missed weeks is often hard because the child feels overwhelmed by the amount of make-up work that is due and feels isolated from his classmates.

If a child misses a lot of school over the years, then she is at risk in the long run for delinquent behavior and dropping out of school. Dropping out of school is obviously a very serious problem because doing so prevents the child from going to college and securing certain jobs. Indeed, studies of adolescents who dropped out of school show that, as adults, they often have economic, marital, and social problems. In addition, many of these adults require treatment for psychological problems such as depression or substance abuse. *However, these consequences do not necessarily apply to everyone who drops out of school.*

What about the effect of school refusal behavior on family members? In the short term, a child's refusal to attend school often leads to chaos, distress, tension, fighting, and endless trips to school to meet with guidance counselors, school psychologists, principals, teachers, and other educators. As a child's attendance problems continue, a family may be faced with legal consequences and financial difficulty if work is missed. A sense of helplessness or despair may set in as well, and some children become less supervised.

Although all seems lost at times, you can get your child to attend school on a regular basis and lower his distress level while there. I must warn you, however, that doing so will take work on your part and your child's part. Following the guidelines in this book should help you accomplish what you want to accomplish. However, keep in mind that success for these kids does not always involve full-time school attendance.

Defining Success

How do you know if this book worked for you? The most obvious way of knowing that it worked is that your child is back in school and attending full-time. In addition, she should be going to school with less distress. However, "success" for kids with school refusal behavior sometimes means different things for different kids. For some older adolescents, for example, especially those with long histories of attendance problems, success means that the teenager is enrolled in a partial credit program, an alternative high school, a credit-by-examination or equivalency diploma program, summer classes, and/or school-based mental health services designed to improve school attendance. If one of these programs helps a child receive a good education and a diploma, then I would consider the program to be a success.

What If I Try the Methods in This Book and Nothing Happens?

If you do try the methods outlined in this book and for whatever reason they do not seem to help, then one of several things might be going on. First, your situation may not completely fit the purpose of this book, so different or more extensive procedures may be necessary; however, the procedures discussed in this book can still be done under the guidance of a qualified mental health professional, who can help you address more intense kinds of issues such as symptoms of attention-deficit/hyperactivity disorder and persistent school refusal behavior.

Second, you may have applied the wrong methods for your child. If you think this is the case, return to chapter 2 and try to see exactly what is maintaining your child's school refusal behavior. Third, you may have tried the methods for only a short time. All of the methods in this book have to be carried out for the entire school year. Some parents get their child back to school and then lose a little focus. Instead, parents usually have to practice the methods in this book for at least several months.

Okay, What's Next?

If you feel this book might be helpful to you and that it seems to apply to your situation, then let's get started! I have a couple of things to ask you to do to set the groundwork for what is to come.

When helping a child get back to school with less distress, frequent communication between parents and school officials is necessary.

Contact Information

The first thing I would like you to do is make a list of relevant names, telephone numbers, and e-mail addresses that you will need. When helping a child get back to school with less distress, frequent communication between parents and school officials is necessary. As such, I would like you to have all contact information at your fingertips. In the worksheet provided, please write the names, main and cell phone numbers, fax numbers, and e-mail addresses for the people listed.

Parent-School Official Discussions

The second thing I would like you to do is to immediately schedule face-to-face meetings with your child's teacher(s) and guidance counselor. You may have already done this, but before using any of the methods in this book I prefer that you do so again and let school officials know what you plan to do. For a child to get back to school with less distress, parents and school officials must be on the same page. In addition, if you have not already done so, please speak with school officials about the following types of information:

- Your child's recent school absences (how many, what type, getting worse or better?)

- Your child's course schedule and grades

- Your child's current homework and required make-up work

- Your child's current behavior in school, including his or her level of distress, interactions with peers and others, and any behavior problems.

- School rules regarding attendance, student conduct, and leaving the school campus during the day

- Expected timeline and obstacles for getting your child back to school

- Legal, disciplinary, and other consequences of continued school absences

Some of this information may be needed only one time, such as school policy about ongoing absences. Still, be sure to write down all of this important information and keep it close to you. Feel free to write this information in the blank pages of this book.

Other types of information change a lot, however, and have to be updated constantly. This mostly applies to homework and makeup work. Therefore, write this information *every week* in the worksheet provided. Feel free to photocopy this worksheet or download multiple copies from the companion Web site at www.oup.com/us/schoolrefusal.

Finally, I have seen many cases of school refusal behavior where parents and school officials do not like each other very much. School refusal behavior often involves a lot of finger pointing and blame. I strongly encourage you

Worksheet 1.1

Contact Information

Me

_____

_____

My spouse/partner

_____

_____

My child (cell phone number most likely)

_____

_____

Close family relatives who live nearby and others (e.g., neighbors, friends) who can help

_____

_____

My child's guidance counselor

_____

_____

My child's teacher(s)

_____

_____

My child's principal/dean

_____

_____

My child's school psychologist or school-based social worker

_____

_____

My child's school nurse

_____

_____

My child's school attendance officer

_____

_____

at this point to work to reduce conflict and friction with school officials as much as possible. Getting a child back to school with less distress has to be a team effort! Members of the team must work together. If friction exists, I recommend that parents and educators communicate often and come to meetings with specific ideas for resolving a child's attendance problem.

On to Chapter 2

Now that you have everyone's contact information and have spoken with school officials, I invite you to begin reading chapter 2. There we discuss ways of discovering exactly what is maintaining your child's trouble attending school. Once we figure that out, we can begin to work to fix the problem.

Different Types of
School Refusal Behavior

In chapter 1 we discussed different kinds of problems that kids may have when attending school. In this chapter, we begin to solve these problems by first:

- Keeping track of, and recording, your child's attendance, level of distress, and morning behavior problems

- Finding out exactly why your child is having trouble attending school so we know which chapters (3 through 6) apply most to you

Tracking and Recording Your Child's School Refusal Behavior

One of the most important things I will ask you to do is keep track of your child's attendance problems. In particular, I will ask you to keep track of your child's actual time in school, level of distress, and morning behavior problems. For the methods in this book to work, you must keep track of your child's behavior *every day*. I ask you to do this for several reasons—knowing about your child's attendance problems each day will help you, your spouse/partner, your child, and school officials to:

> *You must keep track of your child's behavior every day.*

- Become more aware of your child's actual time in school, level of distress, and morning behavior problems

- See how your child's behavior changes during the week

- Find out why your child is having trouble attending school

- See whether the methods in this book that you are trying are indeed working

- Exchange more detailed information with one another

- Look for signs that your child's attendance problems may be recurring after the initial problem was fixed

The most important behaviors that should be recorded each school day include actual time in school (attendance), level of distress about school, and morning behavior problems. Let's discuss these separately.

Actual Time in School

If you are reading this book, then increasing the time your child actually spends in school each day may be one of your most important goals. Therefore, we must know how much time your child actually spends in school each day and whether she is going to school more or less than before. Then we can know whether our goal is being reached and what changes we need to make to improve attendance.

I recognize that you may be unsure about how much time your child actually spends in school each day. Some parents are very familiar with their child's daily attendance because they try to take their child to school each day and see the problems that occur. Other parents are less sure about their child's actual attendance because the child tries to hide behaviors such as skipping classes or ditching school early. Still other parents are completely in the dark about their child's attendance or feel that school officials should be providing them with attendance information. All of these situations are normal, but it's time for a change!

No matter how aware you are now of your child's attendance, *it is very important that you begin to keep track of your child's actual time in school each day.* To do so, you may need the help of others, such as a guidance counselor, teacher, or school attendance officer who can communicate with you daily to let you know whether your child was in school that day. Perhaps you can arrange a daily time for a telephone call with a guidance counselor, have a school official e-mail you each day, or have a daily report card of attendance sent home each day. Although time-consuming, communicating in some way with school officials about your child's attendance *each day* is often crucial so that any problem can be dealt with *immediately*, like that night.

To help you keep track of your child's time in school, use the worksheet that is provided. This is a simple document that involves two recordings. In the first column for each school day, record the number of hours your child actually spent in school. If your child went to school the entire day, then you can mark "all" or "full attendance" in the column. If your child missed a certain amount of school time, then be sure this is recorded. For example, your child may have been expected to go to school on Monday from 9 a.m. to 3 p.m. but did not enter school until 11 a.m. In this case, 4 hours were actually spent in school, so a "4" would be recorded for Monday.

In the second column for each school day, write down whether any partial or full absence from school was *legitimate or excused* ("yes" or "no"). For example, a child may have been truly sick on Tuesday, so a "yes" would be provided in the second column for Tuesday. Be sure to write "yes" *only* if your child was truly sick or was legitimately absent or excused from school for the reasons mentioned in chapter 1 (e.g., medical doctor appointment, family emergency, hazardous weather conditions).

Finally, at the bottom of the worksheet, write the times that your child should enter school in the morning and leave school in the afternoon. Use these times to help you know what percentage of school time your child is missing. If your daughter is missing 2 hours out of every 6-hour school day, for example, then she is absent for 33% of school time. Knowing these morning and afternoon times will also be useful for getting the morning routine under control (see chapter 5) and for checking on your child in the afternoon if she is expected to come home right after school.

You may have a unique situation that does not completely fit this worksheet. For example, your child may go to school every day but have a lot of distress while there. Therefore, every day is marked as "all" or "full attendance." Or your child may stay in the school building but not enter her classroom (in this case, she is actually in the school building, so count this as a "yes" for now). Or your child has been out of school for quite some time, so every day is marked as an absence.

Worksheet 2.1

	No. of hours spent in school	Legitimate absence?
Monday	_____	_____
Tuesday	_____	_____
Wednesday	_____	_____
Thursday	_____	_____
Friday	_____	_____
Monday	_____	_____
Tuesday	_____	_____
Wednesday	_____	_____
Thursday	_____	_____
Friday	_____	_____
Monday	_____	_____
Tuesday	_____	_____
Wednesday	_____	_____
Thursday	_____	_____
Friday	_____	_____
Monday	_____	_____
Tuesday	_____	_____
Wednesday	_____	_____
Thursday	_____	_____
Friday	_____	_____
Monday	_____	_____
Tuesday	_____	_____
Wednesday	_____	_____
Thursday	_____	_____
Friday	_____	_____

What time should my child enter in school in the morning? _____

What time should my child leave school in the afternoon? _____

Despite these situations, I still ask that you complete this worksheet each school day. As you use the methods in this book, you will find that your child's attendance changes. For example, some children go back to school or their classroom very gradually, sometimes hour by hour, so knowing how many hours they did so is very important. In addition, we always want to know as soon as possible whether any problems arise. For example, if your child suddenly misses more school, and you are quickly aware of this because you have been completing the worksheet, then you can more quickly respond to the problem. Feel free to photocopy this worksheet from the book or download multiple copies from the companion Web site at www.oup.com/us/schoolrefusal.

Level of Distress Regarding School

Another important goal that you may have if you are reading this book is to help your child attend school with less distress. Therefore, another important piece of information that you and your child should track each day is your child's level of distress regarding school. "Distress" can refer to your child's level of anxiety, worry, uneasiness, discomfort, nervousness, apprehensiveness, or dread about school. Distress in children is shown in different ways, including crying, clinging, tantrums, irritability, restlessness, withdrawal, and verbal statements about staying home, among other ways. In the space provided below, write down ways you can tell that your child is distressed:

_____

_____

_____

_____

You may use the worksheet provided to record ratings of your child's level of distress about school (worksheet 2.2). You may photocopy this worksheet from the book or download multiple copies from the companion Web site at www.oup.com/us/schoolrefusal. In the first column of the worksheet, write your rating of your child's level of distress about school each day. This can be done on a 0-to-10 scale where 0 is none and 10 is "the worst" (see bottom of worksheet).

Worksheet 2.2

	Your rating of your child's distress *Morning Afternoon Evening*	Your child's rating of his/her distress *Morning Afternoon Evening*
Monday	_____	_____
Tuesday	_____	_____
Wednesday	_____	_____
Thursday	_____	_____
Friday	_____	_____
Saturday	_____	_____
Sunday	_____	_____
Monday	_____	_____
Tuesday	_____	_____
Wednesday	_____	_____
Thursday	_____	_____
Friday	_____	_____
Saturday	_____	_____
Sunday	_____	_____
Monday	_____	_____
Tuesday	_____	_____
Wednesday	_____	_____
Thursday	_____	_____
Friday	_____	_____
Saturday	_____	_____
Sunday	_____	_____

Worksheet 2.2 (continued)

	Your rating of your child's distress			*Your child's rating of his/her distress*		
	Morning	*Afternoon*	*Evening*	*Morning*	*Afternoon*	*Evening*
Monday			_____			_____
Tuesday			_____			_____
Wednesday			_____			_____
Thursday			_____			_____
Friday			_____			_____
Saturday			_____			_____
Sunday			_____			_____
Monday			_____			_____
Tuesday			_____			_____
Wednesday			_____			_____
Thursday			_____			_____
Friday			_____			_____
Saturday			_____			_____
Sunday			_____			_____

X-----X-----X-----X-----X-----X-----X-----X-----X-----X-----X

0	1	2	3	4	5	6	7	8	9	10
None		A little		Some		Stronger		A lot		The worst

In the second column of the worksheet, ask your child to give you a rating of her distress about school that day. Do not influence your child's answer; her rating may be different than your own, and that's okay! Our goal is to get both ratings—yours and your child's—to lower and more manageable levels. If your child wants to keep her ratings on a separate sheet, that is okay. Your child may also want to keep her ratings private, and that is okay as long as you know that she is actually keeping track of her level of distress every day.

In addition, please give separate distress ratings for the morning, afternoon, and evening. Why? Because we want to know the exact pattern of your child's distress during the day so we know exactly how to handle it. All of following patterns of ratings, for example, will be addressed in this book:

- Jennifer is distressed only in the morning before school, so her morning distress ratings are usually higher than for the rest of the day.

- Mark has no problem going to school in the morning but becomes distressed as the day progresses, so his afternoon distress ratings are usually higher than for the rest of the day.

- Zachary is most distressed in the evenings before school, so his evening distress ratings are usually higher than for the rest of the day.

- Sondra is distressed the entire school day, so her ratings usually stay high throughout the day.

You may be asking at this point: What if my child is distressed about only *one* thing? For example, your child may be distressed *only* about riding the school bus, entering the school building, walking into a classroom, speaking to or in front of others, eating in the cafeteria, or walking down school hallways. Or your child may be distressed *only* for a 15-minute period before the start of school. If your child is distressed by only one situation, then provide a distress rating during this situation. For example, if your child is distressed only by having to ride the school bus, then provide a distress rating for the bus ride each day.

You may also be asking: How can I know what my child's level of distress is during the school day? You should be able to rate your child's level of distress in the morning before school and during the evening after school. If you cannot, then talk with others who are around your child during these times and try to make an educated guess about your child's level of distress (or have them provide the rating).

Regarding the afternoon, rate your child's level of distress if she is home from school that afternoon *or* as she arrives home after school. If possible, speak to your child's teacher or guidance counselor *each day* or ask her to send home a "daily report card" of your child's attendance and distress level. A sample daily report card to be completed by school officials is provided. You may photocopy this worksheet from the book or download multiple

---

Worksheet 2.3
Daily Report Card

Date: _____

Number of hours spent in school today _____

Level of distress shown by child today (use 0–10 scale) _____

X-----X-----X-----X-----X-----X-----X-----X-----X-----X-----X

| 0 | 1 | 2 | 3 | 4 | 5 | 6 | 7 | 8 | 9 | 10 |
| None | | A little | | Some | | Stronger | | A lot | | The worst |

Behavior problems in school today

_____

_____

_____

_____

Homework today or other comments

_____

_____

_____

_____

---

copies from the companion Web site at www.oup.com/us/schoolrefusal. You may also have to rely on your child's report of her own distress during the afternoon.

You may also be wondering: Why do I have to give ratings on Saturday and Sunday? A couple of reasons. First, some children say they are very distressed about school even on the weekends, and *this is a strong sign of true distress*. Second, many children report great distress about school on Sunday nights, and we want to be sure we know about this. Some of the methods that I discuss in this book will be necessary even on Saturdays and Sundays.

Finally, you may be asking: What if my child is not distressed about school but simply won't go? I understand that many children refuse school even when they are not distressed (we'll talk about these kids later in this chapter). Some kids skip classes or part of the school day to be with their friends and not because they are distressed. Even in this situation, however, I encourage you and your child to provide the distress ratings each day. As your child goes back to school and needs to stay there for an entire day, she may feel some distress when doing so. The ratings will allow us to see if any distress is present and then we can address it using the methods in this book.

Morning Behavior Problems

Another important goal that you may have if you are reading this book is to help your child attend school with fewer behavior problems in the morning. Therefore, another important topic to keep track of each day is your child's morning behavior problems. Many families of children with school refusal behavior tell me that their morning routine is chaotic, stressful, and full of conflict. Together, we will tackle these problems by making the morning routine more smooth, predictable, and stress-free. First, however, we have to know what we are up against.

Children with trouble attending school often show several behavior problems in the morning. You will see a list of these behavior problems in worksheet 2.4. If your child shows any of these behaviors in the morning on a particular weekday (Monday through Friday), then place a checkmark next to them. For example, if your child was particularly clingy on

Monday, then place a checkmark next to "clings to an adult" in the Monday column. *Do this each day* and place as many checkmarks as apply for that day. You may photocopy this worksheet from the book or download multiple copies from the companion Web site at www.oup.com/us/schoolrefusal. If your child shows one or two unique morning behavior problems that are not listed on the worksheet, then please write them in the space below:

_____

_____

_____

_____

Add these behavior problems to the blank lines on worksheet 2.4. If your child has no morning behavior problems, then this worksheet is not necessary. Your child may, for example, go to school in the morning with no problem but skip classes during the day. Or she may go to school just fine but is then anxious during classes and tries to come home. These problems will be better measured using worksheets 2.1 (attendance) and 2.2 (level of distress).

Okay, What's Next?

Please get started *right away* completing the worksheets about your child's actual time spent in school, level of distress, and morning behavior problems. Again, please complete worksheets *every day* and save them in a binder or folder. As we discuss methods of getting your child to attend school with less distress, we will refer to these worksheets to see if the methods are working. However, completing these worksheets now does not mean we have to wait to do

> *Complete worksheets every day and save them in a binder or folder.*

something about your child's attendance problem. We can move straight ahead to discovering the exact reason why your child is having trouble going to school. Let's do that now.

	Monday	Tuesday	Wednesday	Thursday	Friday
Refuses to/cannot get out of bed	_____	_____	_____	_____	_____
Refuses to move	_____	_____	_____	_____	_____
Will not get ready for school	_____	_____	_____	_____	_____
Locks self in room or car	_____	_____	_____	_____	_____
Cries a lot	_____	_____	_____	_____	_____
Temper tantrum	_____	_____	_____	_____	_____
Excessive dawdling	_____	_____	_____	_____	_____
Clings to an adult	_____	_____	_____	_____	_____
Stomachache or other complaint	_____	_____	_____	_____	_____
Runs away from home or school	_____	_____	_____	_____	_____
_____	_____	_____	_____	_____	_____
_____	_____	_____	_____	_____	_____
Refuses to/cannot get out of bed	_____	_____	_____	_____	_____
Refuses to move	_____	_____	_____	_____	_____
Will not get ready for school	_____	_____	_____	_____	_____
Locks self in room or car	_____	_____	_____	_____	_____
Cries a lot	_____	_____	_____	_____	_____
Temper tantrum	_____	_____	_____	_____	_____
Excessive dawdling	_____	_____	_____	_____	_____
Clings to an adult	_____	_____	_____	_____	_____

Worksheet 2.4 (continued)

	Monday	Tuesday	Wednesday	Thursday	Friday
Stomachache or other complaint	____	____	____	____	____
Runs away from home or school	____	____	____	____	____
_____	____	____	____	____	____
_____	____	____	____	____	____
Refuses to/cannot get out of bed	____	____	____	____	____
Refuses to move	____	____	____	____	____
Will not get ready for school	____	____	____	____	____
Locks self in room or car	____	____	____	____	____
Cries a lot	____	____	____	____	____
Temper tantrum	____	____	____	____	____
Excessive dawdling	____	____	____	____	____
Clings to an adult	____	____	____	____	____
Stomachache or other complaint	____	____	____	____	____
Runs away from home or school	____	____	____	____	____
_____	____	____	____	____	____
_____	____	____	____	____	____

Knowing Why Your Child Has Trouble
Going to School

Children show many different behaviors when refusing school (see chapter 1), which can make the problem seem so frustrating and overwhelming. Isn't there an easier way of thinking about this problem? Yes, there is! A simpler way of looking at school refusal behavior is to concentrate on why your child has trouble attending school. In other words, why is your child continuing to show problems going to school? Helping you find the answer to this question and then figuring out what to do next are my goals for the rest of this chapter.

I have found that children generally have trouble going to school for one or more of four main reasons. Focusing on these four reasons is much easier than focusing on the many different behavior problems your child may be showing. Once we find out which of these reasons most applies to your child, I can better point you to which direction you should take to resolve your child's attendance problem. Please start thinking about which of these reasons seems to most apply to *your child:*

- To get away from general school-related situations that cause distress

- To get away from school-related social/performance situations that cause distress

- To get attention from significant others such as parents

- To get to do fun activities outside of school

General School-Related Situations That Cause Distress

Younger children often have trouble going to school because some general school-related situation causes distress for them. Some children are able to say what causes their distress, and some parents can easily tell what causes their child's distress. Distress is sometimes related to:

- The school bus or car ride to school or getting sick during the bus or car ride

- Missing the school bus

- Entering the school building or classroom

- A particular teacher or other school official

- A particular class or area such as the playground

- Peers/classmates

- Moving from one area of the school building to another, such as from a classroom to physical education class

- School cafeteria

- Animals, fire alarm, or other specific item

In most cases of distress, children do not or cannot say specifically what is bothering them. This is very common. Parents and school officials are sometimes frustrated by a child's school refusal behavior because the child cannot say exactly what causes her distress. As a result, parents and others ask endless questions that lead nowhere or they have trouble believing that the child is actually distressed.

Your child may be unable to say exactly what is bothering her about school. Why? First, your child may not able to fully describe what it is that bothers her. Some children only know that they "feel bad" at school and do not want to be there. In other words, they are truly distressed about school but lack the ability to describe why in detail. This is normal for young children.

Second, your child may be truly distressed about being in school but for no particular reason. Again, this is normal for young children and we can work to lower your child's distress even without knowing exactly what it is that bothers her. If you are constantly asking your child to tell you what is wrong and she cannot say, then it is okay to stop asking these questions.

Children with trouble attending school because they are distressed are usually younger, about 5 to 10 years of age. However, any school-age child could have trouble attending school because of distress. In addition, these children often (though not always) show the following behaviors in the morning and sometimes during the school day:

- Crying or tearfulness

- Anxiety or nervousness

- Sadness or withdrawal from others (usually nervousness and sadness occur together in these children and are hard to tease apart)

- Crankiness, irritability, restlessness, and muscle tension

- Trouble concentrating or sleeping because of school-related distress

- Verbal statements about not wanting to go to school and "hating" it there

- Physical complaints such as stomachaches, headaches, nausea, or other symptoms (see chapter 1)

- Voice or hands shaking

- Pleas with parents for home schooling, excused absences, or future nonattendance

- Fear of some specific school-related object or situation, such as an animal

What attendance patterns do these kids usually show? Some children who are distressed about school do in fact go to school but remain distressed while there. For some of these children, their level of distress eventually goes down as the school day wears on, but others remain distressed for most of the school day. Other children become very distressed once their parents bring them to school, and they refuse to enter the school building. Some of these kids will eventually go to school following a battle to get them in the school building, and others will put up such a fuss that they are able to stay home from school. Finally, many of these children remain truly distressed about school even on Saturday and Sunday, and especially Sunday evening.

Consider, for example, the case of Joseph:

Joseph is a 7-year-old boy who dawdles in the morning and complains almost every day that he does not want to go to school. He gets up slowly, immediately complains of having a stomachache, cries during the morning, and takes a long time to get dressed. His mother can eventually get him into the car to go to school, but once Joseph is on the school playground with his mother he sobs and says, "I hate school." Despite questions from his mother and his teacher about why he hates school, Joseph only shrugs and says, "I just don't want to go!" In addition, Joseph recently has been complaining at night about going to school. This seems especially the case on Sunday evenings.

If Joseph reminds you of your child, then she may be having problems going to school to get away from distress that is felt there. Many of these children are not so concerned about being home as they are about being away from school.

Keep in mind that the distress I am talking about here is not related to any legitimate reason for missing school. For example, if a child is distressed about school because a bully is threatening her, then the distress is understandable and the threat must be resolved before any of the methods in this book are used (see chapter 1). In addition, your child's distress should be much worse than what is seen for most kids of her age. Compare your child to other kids of her age and see whether her distress about school is much worse than theirs. If so, then the methods in this book will be more helpful.

I am referring to children who are *truly* distressed about school and who have trouble going to school even though there is no real reason to feel distressed. If you feel very confident that this reason for school refusal behavior most applies to your child, then the methods discussed in chapter 3 will be most helpful for you. If you are less sure, however, or feel that other reasons may apply (which may be the case), then please keep reading.

School-Related Social/Performance Situations That Cause Distress

Although younger children often cannot say exactly what causes them so much distress at school, older children and adolescents often can. When older children and adolescents are distressed about school, it is often because of social or performance situations at school that are difficult for them. In particular, they worry about making mistakes or being embarrassed or humiliated in front of other people. Some kids worry about being teased, laughed at, or ignored by others. Other kids worry about becoming sick, vomiting, choking, blushing, urinating, or fainting before others. Many of these kids shrink from social and performance situations where they might become the center of attention.

What do I mean by social and performance situations? *Social situations* include interactions with others. *Performance situations* include acting in some way before others. Both kinds of situations can make children very nervous or distressed. Some common *social situations* at school that cause children distress include:

- Starting or maintaining a conversation with other kids or adults, especially people the child does not know well

- Joining a conversation that others are having or introducing oneself

- Asking a teacher or other authority figures for help

- Interacting with others in a school hallway

- Playing with others on a playground

- Working with other children on a group project

- Participating in group, team, or club meetings

- Being at assemblies or other large crowds or gatherings at school

- Answering or talking on the telephone

- Setting up dates or get-togethers with peers

Some common *performance situations* at school that cause children distress include:

- Speaking or reading in front of others in class, such as giving an oral presentation

- Volunteering an answer or having to answer a teacher's question in class

- Writing on the blackboard in front of others, such as solving a math problem

- Taking tests or completing other tasks that will be graded

- Performing in physical education class at school

- Undressing before others in a locker room

- Performing musically in front of others, such as singing or playing an instrument

- Driving before others, as in driving class

- Eating in a cafeteria with others who might be watching the child eat

- Using the restrooms at school

- Walking into school or class when others might be watching

- Participating in social events such as school dances or extracurricular activities

- Having one's picture taken

Children with trouble attending school because they want to get away from distressing social or performance situations are usually older, about 11 to 17 years of age. However, any school-age child could have trouble attending school because of distressing social or performance situations. In addition, these children often (though not always) show the following behaviors throughout the school day:

- Particular anxiety about one class or section of the school day

- Nervousness when around others or when expected to do something in front of others

- Excessive worry about making mistakes or being embarrassed or humiliated

- Skipping particular classes, such as physical education or math class

- Skipping a particular class on a day when a test, oral presentation, or other assignment in front of others is scheduled

- Asking for course schedule changes

- Avoiding situations that involve interactions with others (such avoidance may be obvious, such as eating lunch in the bathroom, or more subtle, such as eating lunch very near the door of the cafeteria so a quick exit can be made if distress becomes intense)

- Failure to hand in homework or other school assignments because they are not perfect

What attendance patterns do these kids usually show? Some children who are distressed about social or performance situations do in fact go to school but remain distressed while there. Other children tend to skip only those classes that make them most anxious, such as physical education class. Still other children ditch school for whole sections of the day, such as after lunch, or for the entire day.

Consider, for example, the case of Tyanna:

Tyanna is a 14-year-old girl who has trouble going to school most days because she feels lonely and isolated at school. Being new to this school district, Tyanna has been slow to make friends and often seems uncomfortable in situations where she has to speak up at school. In particular, Tyanna seems to have a hard time answering questions in class and talking with others. Tyanna says she often feels embarrassed at school and that "everything I do is wrong." She is generally shy and has been skipping her physical education class because she does not want to get undressed before others. Tyanna's parents say their daughter is often sad and anxious on school days but seems fine on weekends.

If Tyanna reminds you of your child, then your child may be having problems going to school because she wants to get away from distressing social or performance situations there. Many of these children are not so eager to be home as they are to be away from school.

Keep in mind that the social and performance distress I am talking about here is *not related to any legitimate reason for missing school.* For example, if a child is distressed about school because someone is threatening her, then the distress is understandable and the threat must be resolved before any of the methods in this book are used (see chapter 1). In addition, your child's social or performance distress should be much worse than what is seen for most kids his or her age. Compare your child to other kids her age and see whether her distress about social or performance situations is much worse than theirs. If so, then the methods in this book will be more helpful.

I am referring to children who are *truly* distressed about social or performance situations at school and who have trouble going to school even though there is no real reason to feel distressed. If you feel *very confident* that this reason for school refusal behavior most applies to your child, then the methods discussed in chapter 4 will be most helpful for you. If you are less sure, however, or feel that other reasons may apply (which may be the case), then please keep reading.

You may have noticed that the first two reasons I discussed for missing school are similar because both involve some level of distress. This means that these children are having trouble attending school because they *want to get away from something at school* that is causing them distress. Your child may be having trouble going to school for *both* of the reasons discussed so far, and that is okay. If you feel *very confident* that this is the case, then chapters 3 *and* 4 will be helpful to you.

Other children, however, are not so concerned about getting away from something distressing at school as they are *getting something positive outside of school*. In particular, many children have trouble attending school because they want attention from their parents or because they want to do fun things outside of school. Let's talk about these two reasons next.

To Get Attention From Significant Others

Younger children sometimes have trouble going to school because they much prefer to be with parents at their home or work. These children may or may not be distressed about school but are much more concerned about being home from school to get attention from their parents. Many children, for example, want to help their parents care for a new baby, complete chores around the house, or go to work with their parents.

Children with trouble attending school because they want attention from their parents are usually younger, about 5 to 10 years of age. However, any school-age child could have trouble attending school because she wants attention from parents. In addition, these children often (though not always) show the following behaviors throughout the school day:

- Defiance about going to school in the morning, often in the form of temper tantrums

- Stubborn, willful, manipulative, or guilt-inducing behavior to try to stay home

- Verbal statements about wanting to stay home

- Desires for parent to attend school with the child or eat lunch with the child

- Constant telephone calls to parents during the school day

- Constant questions about when a parent will pick up the child from school

- Need for reassurance from parents about the consequences of being separated

- Running away from the school building to try to get home

Many of these children do not say they "hate school" and are more concerned about being with their parents. Indeed, many of these kids would gladly go to school if their parents went with them! In addition, many of these kids seek attention from their parents in other ways. For example, some children put up a fuss when left with a babysitter, when asked to sleep over at another child's house, or when invited to be at a friend's birthday party without their parents present. Some kids even have trouble sleeping by themselves or being on a floor of the house separate from their parents.

What kind of attendance patterns do these kids usually show? Many of these kids will miss at least part of the school day, usually in the morning as they try their hardest to stay home. As a result, many have a lot of "tardys" or days where they come in late to school. Many times these kids "settle down" after a while in school and attend without any problems the rest of the day. In other cases, though, the child puts up such a fuss that she is able to stay home from school on a particular day. A more serious problem is a child who goes to school but then runs away from the school building at some point during the day to try to be near home.

Some children who seek attention from their parents also worry about something harmful happening to their parents. Many of these kids, for example, worry that their parents will be in a car accident that prevents the child from seeing them again. Others worry that something bad will happen to their parents and the child will be stranded at school. Sometimes, though not always, these concerns follow some major change in the household, such as a parent's illness or hospitalization, minor traffic accident, move to a new area, or fighting or separation or divorce between the parents. In addition, these children feel they often have to "check in" with their parents to be sure that nothing bad has happened to their mom or dad.

Other children who seek attention from their parents also worry about something harmful happening to themselves. Many of these kids, for example, worry that they will be kidnapped at school and never see their parents again. Some of these kids may have nightmares about being away from their parents or away from home. In addition, they feel they often have to "check in" with their parents to say that nothing bad has happened to them.

This description implies that a child is distressed, but the distress is more about separation from parents and less about school. However, these kids are *not necessarily* distressed about separating from their parents. Instead, many are *defiant and oppositional* in their behavior to try to be home with their parents.

Consider, for example, the case of Emily:

Emily is a 6-year-old girl who has trouble going to school most days because she would rather be with her mother at home. Emily has just entered first grade and seems upset that she has to go an entire school day without seeing her mom. She cries in the morning before school and stomps her feet, asking, "Why can't I just stay home?" Her mother says that getting Emily to school is a daily problem because Emily is "so stubborn and hard to control." Therefore, Emily's mother started missing some work to volunteer to help in Emily's classroom just so the morning routine is a little easier. However, Emily's mother is worried that she is missing too much work and will soon have to stop going to class with her daughter.

If Emily reminds you of your child, then your child may be having problems going to school because she wants attention from you and/or your spouse/partner. Again, many of these children are not so concerned about school as they are about being home with at least one parent.

Keep in mind that the attention-getting behavior I am talking about here is *not related to any legitimate reason for missing school*. For example, if you are in the middle of a difficult custody dispute and your child has legitimate worries about what will happen next, then this situation must be resolved *before* any of the methods in this book are used. In addition, *your child's attention-seeking behavior should be much worse than what is seen for most kids her age*. Compare your child to other kids her age and see whether her attention-seeking behavior is much worse than theirs. If so, then the methods in this book will be more helpful.

I am referring to children who are *truly* seeking attention from their parents and who have trouble going to school even though there is no legitimate reason for doing so. If you feel *very confident* that this reason for school refusal behavior most applies to *your child*, then the methods discussed in chapter 5 will be most helpful for you. If you are less sure, however, or feel that another reason may apply (which may be the case), then please keep reading.

To Get to Do Fun Activities Outside School

Older children and adolescents sometimes have trouble going to school because they would much rather be doing fun activities outside school. These children are not particularly distressed about school, though they may say they are bored there. In addition, these children usually *do not* want attention from their parents or even want them to know they are out of school! Many children have trouble attending school, for example, because they would much rather be:

- Sleeping late

- Watching television, playing videogames, talking on the telephone, or chatting on the Internet at home

- Playing games or sports with friends who are also missing school

- Riding their bike

- Hanging out alone or with friends at a restaurant, shopping center, or mall

- Eating somewhere away from the school campus

- Joyriding in a car

- Attending day parties with peers who are also missing school

- Working at a job

Children who have trouble attending school because they would rather do fun activities outside of school are usually older, about 11 to 17 years of age. However, any school-age child could refuse school to do fun activities outside school. In addition, these children often (though not always) show the following behaviors during the day:

- Skipping classes or large parts of the school day without anyone knowing

- Hanging out with friends who tempt the child to miss school

- Fighting with parents or others so the absences can continue

- Boredom at school or lack of motivation

- Constant requests of parents to drop out of school or get a job

- Breaking curfew

What kind of attendance patterns do these kids usually show? Most of these kids will miss at least part of the school day to pursue the fun things they want to do. This may mean skipping school altogether, or playing "hooky" Tom Sawyer–style! Other kids will skip classes after lunch or mid-morning and miss the rest of the day. Many of these kids choose to eat lunch off campus and then decide to take the rest of the day off! In general, they do not want anyone to know where they are, except of course their friends.

These kinds of attendance problems are different and more serious than simple "senioritis," where an adolescent close to graduation skips a few classes because of lack of motivation and because the consequences for skipping are not strong ("I'm going to graduate anyway!"). Instead, I am talking about a situation where graduation is nowhere in sight and the child specifically wants to miss school to be with friends or do fun activities outside of school. As a result, his or her absenteeism is serious.

Consider, for example, the case of Vincent:

Vincent is a 16-year-old boy who was reported by his school for missing much of the past 2 weeks of school. Vincent usually goes to school in the morning but often leaves right before or right after lunch. When asked why, Vincent says that his "friends" come up to him at his locker and urge him to ditch school with them. Vincent says he feels obligated to go and somewhat guilty at the time, but then has a good time with his friends during the after-

noon. Lately, though, Vincent has been leaving his house in the morning and going straight to a friend's house. His grades are started to fall.

Does Vincent remind you of your child? If so, then your child may be having problems going to school because she wants to do more fun activities outside of school. Many of these kids are not distressed about school and certainly do not want much attention from their parents. They are usually more interested in being with their peers and are not too concerned about the consequences of missing school.

If you feel *very confident* that your child is missing school *only* to do more fun things outside of school, then the methods discussed in chapter 6 will be most helpful for you. However, many children who refuse school to do fun things outside of school do become distressed when they eventually have to go back to school. Therefore, some of the methods discussed in chapters 3 and 4 may be useful in this situation. If you are less sure at this point about why your child has trouble attending school, or feel that more than one reason may apply (which may be the case), then please keep reading.

School Refusal Behavior for More Than One Reason

As you looked through these descriptions of children with trouble attending school, I hope you found one that seems to apply most to your child. If you feel that your child is refusing school for more than one of these reasons, however, that's okay! Many children do in fact have trouble going to school for different reasons. Consider, for example, the following cases:

- Justine is distressed about school and refuses to go, and is allowed to stay home from school. She then realizes all the wonderful things that she can do while at home, like play videogames! Justine is now having trouble attending school because of school-related distress (the first reason we discussed) *and* because she enjoys fun activities outside of school (the fourth reason we discussed).

- Armando has been missing a lot of school to be with friends outside of school (the fourth reason we discussed). His parents are now trying to get him to go back to school, but he is nervous about (1) facing new classmates and teachers ("They'll wonder where I was and ask a million questions!") and (2) having to finish all the make-up work that has piled up (school-related distress, the first reason we discussed).

■ Jessica's parents have recently divorced and Jessica has been refusing school lately so she can be with her mother at home (the third reason we discussed). Jessica is often described as a shy, reserved child who has trouble making friends at school. In fact, she says she does not like school because people try to talk to her and that makes her nervous (the second reason we discussed).

■ Kong has been having a lot of trouble going to school and staying there for a whole day. He says that he is often upset at school but cannot say why (the first reason we discussed). In addition, Kong has trouble being away from his parents and says that he wants to stay home and play (the third and fourth reasons we discussed).

All of these kids have trouble going to school for *more than one reason*. Again, this is common and still fixable! If your child does seem to be having trouble going to school for more than one reason, then I strongly encourage you to read *all* of the chapters in this book.

Okay, What's Next?

Please start tracking and recording your child's actual time in school, level of distress about school, and morning behavior problems on the worksheets in this chapter. *Be sure to do this every day.*

Now we start the hard work of getting your child to go to school with less distress. Please note that the methods in this book will work only if everyone—you, your spouse/partner, your child, *and* your child's guidance counselor and other school officials—put in a lot of effort and work together. Now:

■ If you are *very confident* that your child is having trouble attending school *only* to get away from school-related distress, then chapter 3 will be most helpful to you and I encourage you to start there.

- If you are *very confident* that your child is having trouble attending school *only* to get away from distressing social and performance situations there, then chapter 4 will be most helpful to you and I encourage you to start there.

- If you are *very confident* that your child is having trouble attending school *only* to get attention from you or significant others, then chapter 5 will be most helpful to you and I encourage you to start there.

- If you are *very confident* that your child is having trouble attending school *only* to do fun activities outside of school, then chapter 6 will be most helpful to you and I encourage you to start there.

- If you are still *unsure* as to why your child is having trouble attending school, then carefully reread this chapter or read chapters 3 through 6. You may find in those chapters some additional material that helps you decide which reason for refusing school applies most to your child. You can then use the methods in one or more of those chapters that apply most to you and your child.

Special Topics

Parents often have questions about special topics that will be covered in different chapters. Some of these, such as dealing with threatening situations at school, switching schools, making the transition to a new school, and dealing with conflict with school officials, were presented in chapter 1. Other special topics include:

- Should I medicate my child? (chapter 3)

- Home schooling (chapter 3)

- When should I keep my child home from school? (chapter 3)

- My child won't ride the school bus! (chapter 3)

- Those Sunday evening blues (chapter 3)

- What is a panic attack? (chapter 4)

- Being teased (chapter 4)

- My child is a perfectionist! (chapter 4)

- Gym class (chapter 4)

- Extracurricular activities (chapter 4)

- Returning to school after a break or holiday (chapter 5)

- Should I skip work to go to school with my child? (chapter 5)

- My child is home from school: What now? (chapter 5)

- Calling the police (chapter 6)

- Nothing motivates my child! (chapter 6)

- Problems getting out of bed (chapter 6)

- 504 plans and individualized education plans (chapter 6)

- Alternative school placements (chapter 6)

- Other special circumstances (leaving work before your child has to go to school, multiple children refusing to go to school, children with developmental disorders) (chapter 7)

Children Who Refuse School

to Avoid General Distress

Caleb is a 7-year-old boy who gets up in the morning and immediately starts to cry and say, "I don't want to go to school." Although his parents can get Caleb ready for school, their son sulks during the car ride, complains of having a stomachache, and sobs when he sees the school playground. Caleb's mother says she has a hard time getting her son to go into the school building and that she sometimes drives him home when he seems so distraught. Caleb seems fine once home but sulks as well during the evening before school.

This chapter will be *more helpful* to you if your child matches Caleb's situation or if one or both of the following is true:

- Your child is having trouble going to school in the morning because of distress about school or trouble riding the school bus.

- Your child seems quite distressed in the mornings or evenings before school.

This chapter will be *less helpful* to you if one or both of the following is true:

- Your child is not distressed about school.

- Your child is refusing school *only* for attention (see chapter 5).

- Your child is refusing school *only* to do more fun activities outside of school (see chapter 6).

Children Who Refuse School to Avoid General Distress

In chapter 2 we discussed different reasons why children have trouble going to school. One reason is that some children, like Caleb, want to get away from distress they feel when at school. A child's distress may be due to specific things such as the school bus or walking from one part of the school to another. In many cases, children cannot say what is bothering them, and that's okay. Unless there is some clear threat to your child at school, such as a bully, we do not need to know exactly what is causing his distress. The most important thing is to focus on understanding and reducing the distress and getting your child back in school. Reducing stress and improving school attendance will therefore be the focus of this chapter.

Many children with school-related distress are young (like Caleb) or are going to a new school building for the first time. To help your child improve his school attendance and lower distress, I will concentrate in this chapter on the following:

- Understanding what distress is: the "feeling," "thinking," and "doing" parts of distress

- Lowering physical "feelings" of distress through correct breathing and relaxation

- Dealing with the "thinking" part of distress, or what to do when your child says he doesn't want to go to school

- Managing the "doing" part of distress by gradually reintroducing a child to school and increasing his time in the classroom

Why Am I Doing This?

If your child resembles Caleb, my guess is that he is pretty distressed about going to school at some time during the school day. Your child may be distressed in the morning before school, upon entering the school building, or for most of the school day. Or he is most distressed about school in the evening before the next school day, especially on Sunday evening. We will cover each of these problems in this chapter.

To tackle your child's distress, both you and your child should fully understand what distress actually is. Distress can seem overwhelming and uncontrollable, but the problem can actually be broken down into smaller parts that are easier to understand and control. This will be our first step. Once you know exactly what kind of distress your child has, then we can work to lower his distress and go back to school.

Many distressed children like Caleb have uncomfortable physical feelings such as aches, trembling, shaking, "butterflies in the stomach," and shortness of breath or hyperventilation (breathing too quickly). To help ease these feelings, we will concentrate on breathing and relaxation techniques that your child can use when upset. These exercises are quick, painless, and easy to use. Many children say they feel more comfortable when they have a way of controlling feelings of distress.

Another major focus of this chapter will be gradually increasing the amount of time your child spends in school and in the classroom. There are many different ways of doing this, and we will cover all of these ways so you can find which one will most help your child. Remember that the main goals of this chapter are to help your child be more comfortable about going to school and to stay in school for the entire day. Let's talk next about what distress actually is.

What Is Distress?

You may recall from chapter 2 that "distress" can refer to your child's level of anxiety, worry, uneasiness, discomfort, nervousness, apprehensiveness, or dread about school. Distress in children is shown in different ways, including crying, clinging, tantrums, irritability, restlessness, withdrawal, and verbal statements asking to stay home, among other ways. Your child may also have a unique way of showing his distress, and you may remember that I asked you to write a description of this in chapter 2.

Distress or anxiety is made up of *three main parts*. As you read through each of these parts, think about your description of your child's distress to see which parts apply most to him:

- A "feelings" part that involves uncomfortable physical problems such as aches, trembling, shaking, "butterflies in the stomach," and shortness of breath or hyperventilation (breathing too quickly)

- A "thinking" part that involves uncomfortable thoughts or worries about bad things happening, such as worrying that the school bus will crash or that everyone will laugh during an oral presentation at school. In young children, this part may be shown through statements such as "I don't like school" or "I don't want to go to school."

- A "doing" part that usually involves avoiding places that cause distress, such as staying away from school or withdrawing from people at a birthday party

Do these parts look familiar to you or your child? Let's talk about each one in more detail.

The "Feelings" Part of Distress

My guess is that your child is somewhat nervous about school and that he cries or says "I feel bad" when having to go to school. Many times parents or teachers will ask a child a lot of questions about what is bothering the child about school but come away with little information. Part of the reason for this is that *the child is focusing a lot on how he feels inside.* For whatever reason, school has become associated with uncomfortable physical feelings, and your child may be upset mostly with those feelings. In Caleb's case, for example, he simply couldn't say what was bothering him about school, but he did complain about feeling terrible when there.

An important thing for you and your child to remember is that everyone feels uncomfortable or distressed from time to time—that's part of being human! For example, think about situations where you might feel uncomfortable, such as having to confront a cranky coworker or return merchandise at a store. Most people who are distressed in a certain situation are able to control their distress and move forward with what they have to do. For example, you may go ahead and ask your coworker what is wrong or become assertive when returning an item to the store.

Other people, however, have trouble controlling their distress and moving forward. Such trouble affected Caleb and is affecting your child at this

Should I Medicate My Child?

Some children have such high levels of distress that their parents wonder whether medication, or drug therapy, is a good option. *First and foremost, if you are considering medication for your child's distress, be sure to consult with a child psychiatrist who is familiar with the literature on medications for child anxiety and depression.* Several studies have shown that medication can be effective for some children with high levels of distress, and your child may benefit from one of these medications. These medications are designed to help ease a child's physical "feelings" of distress.

That said, there are some downsides to medication. First, some children with distress do not benefit from medication. Children whose distress is mild or moderate, for example, may not benefit as much from medication as children whose distress is severe. Remember that this book will be more helpful if your child's level of distress is mild or moderate, not severe. Second, side effects from medication may occur. Third, medication may help ease physical "feelings" of distress but may not ease the "thinking" or "doing" parts of distress. This means that a child who takes medication for distress about school may feel physically better, but he or she may still have thoughts about not wanting to go to school or may still try to avoid school.

If you are considering medication for your child, or if you have additional questions about the issues raised here, be sure to speak with a qualified child psychiatrist and clinical child psychologist (see chapter 1). Medication and psychological treatment together are sometimes the best way to treat severe distress in children.

point. Therefore, we have to teach your child ways to control uncomfortable feelings and to move forward toward full-time school attendance.

A reminder: if your child is distressed about some legitimate threat at school, the methods in this chapter will be less helpful to you. If he is distressed about the possibility of being attacked or bullied, for example, *then this threat must be resolved first.* If a true threat has been removed and your child is *still* having trouble going to school, then the methods in this chapter may be more helpful.

> Be sure to keep track of your child's level of distress each day.

Be sure to keep track of your child's level of distress each day by using the worksheet provided in chapter 2. If you like, you can give a rating for each part of distress: the "feelings" part, the "thinking" part, and the "doing" part. Or you can simply give one rating that involves all of these together. As you and your child practice the methods in this chapter, I will ask you to check whether the methods are working by looking at the daily distress ratings. Don't forget to record daily attendance and any morning behavior problems as well!

The "Thinking" Part of Distress

Another important part of distress is the "thinking" part. When we are distressed or anxious about something, we sometimes think about worst-case scenarios. For example, if a family member is late coming home from school or work, we may start to worry that he was in a car accident. This is a normal human experience and one that is usually not a problem: we understand that the worst-case scenario is not likely to have happened. For example, we may shake our head and realize that the odds of the person actually being in a car accident are small and that other explanations are more reasonable, such as getting caught in heavy traffic.

However, some people who are distressed focus a lot on the worst-case scenario and have trouble thinking about other explanations. This also applies to children and adolescents and perhaps to your child now. For example, a teenage boy might assume that others are staring at his skin complexion and laughing as a result. However, the others are likely snickering at something else. This kind of assumption is not unusual but can be a problem if other thoughts are "pushed away." For example, if the teenager does not think about more reasonable explanations for others' laughter, such as the possibility that others are simply responding to a joke, then he is likely to feel embarrassed or distressed.

Think about when this happens to you. What might you think when a coworker won't speak to you one day? Might you assume that he is angry with you? Sure! But most people also consider other possibilities, such as the possibility that the person is having a bad day or is stressed about work and has little time for socializing. When we consider these other explanations, we usually feel better.

Younger children who are distressed *tend not* to have clear thoughts about what distresses them. Despite a lot of parent and teacher questions, these children are not quite able to say what they are thinking in different situations like going to school. Much of this is due to the child's age—he is simply not at a developmental level where much detail can be given about distressing thoughts. Instead, only general statements such as "I don't like school" or "I feel bad in school" are usually given. Such was the case with Caleb. If this is all you can get from your child, don't be overly concerned. There are ways that you can respond to these statements, and we will discuss these ways later in the chapter.

I will cover the "thinking" part of distress more in chapter 4 when discussing older children and adolescents who are distressed about social and performance situations at school. Older children and adolescents tend to have more detailed thoughts than younger children, so different methods can be used. If your child is younger and this chapter is more appropriate, feel free to read chapter 4 anyway; your child will be an adolescent someday!

The "Doing" Part of Distress

The final part of distress is the "doing" part, or what a child actually does when feeling upset. Most kids who are distressed about school, like Caleb, "do" cry, withdraw from others, and try to avoid school. Other kids, though, might throw temper tantrums, scream, and run away from school or home (for this specific problem, see chapter 5). In most cases, crying and time missed from school are what bother parents the most, so I will concentrate on these problems later in this chapter.

As mentioned in chapter 2, avoiding school because of distress is most common in the morning and especially as a child has to walk into the school building and classroom. However, many kids also avoid the school bus or school playground right before school starts. I will cover all these situations.

Your Child's Distress

What does your child "feel," "think" (or say), and "do" when distressed about school? In the spaces below, write your child's specific feelings, thoughts (or statements), and behaviors when he is distressed about school. If your child does not have one of these parts, such as the "thinking" part, then go ahead and leave that part blank.

What my child "feels" when distressed

_____

_____

_____

_____

What my child "thinks" (or says) when distressed

_____

_____

_____

_____

What my child "does" when distressed

_____

_____

_____

_____

All the Parts Together

How do all of these parts of distress tie together? In general, one part of distress often leads to another. In other words, there is usually some sequence to the parts, and this is likely true for your child as well. When we are distressed, for example, we often have unpleasant feelings and thoughts. These unpleasant feelings and thoughts can then lead to behaviors that cause problems. In Caleb's case, for example, he had an unpleasant stomachache (feeling part) and statements about not wanting to go to school (thinking part). The feeling and thinking parts then led to trouble entering the school building (doing part).

As another example, think about someone who is nervous about going to the dentist, like you or me (figure 3.1). Someone who is nervous about the dentist may start to feel physically sick (nauseated, achy) about an hour

Figure 3.1
Distress diagram (dentist)

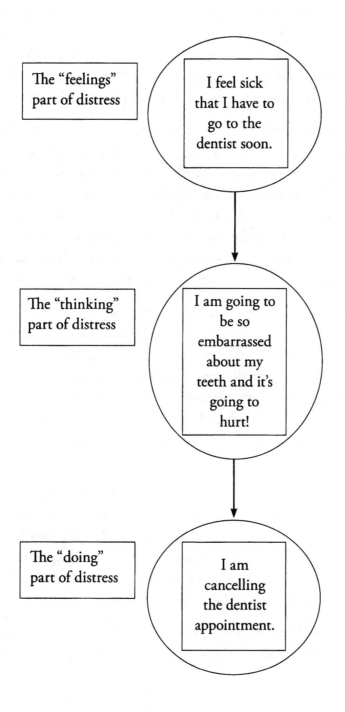

before a dental appointment. These are the physical "feelings" of distress. As these feelings worsen, the person may start to think about all the terrible things that could happen at the dentist's office, such as pain or others' comments about the person's teeth. These thoughts are the "thinking" part of distress. As these physical feelings and worrisome thoughts get worse, the person may be more tempted to cancel the appointment. If the appointment is cancelled, this is the "doing" part of distress.

As soon as the appointment is cancelled, how do you suppose the person feels? Much better, right? Avoiding something works well in the short term because we feel better: the distress has been taken away! But is this a good long-term strategy? No. Sooner or later we have to go to the dentist, and putting it off for a while only makes things worse. The same is true for your child's distress about school. Avoiding school might seem like a good short-term thing to do, because distress is lowered, but eventually your child has to learn to cope with stress and go to school.

Think about how you described your child's distress in the morning. What part of the distress starts first? For many children, the "feelings" part starts first (figure 3.2). For example, a child may wake up with a stomachache or start to feel generally achy or miserable. As these feelings worsen, the child may begin to say things like, "I don't like school" or "I don't want to go to school." At a basic level, these statements are the "thinking" part of distress. As the feelings and statements continue, or get worse, the child may try to avoid school (the "doing" part).

Other children show other patterns of distress (figure 3.3). For example, some children wake up and *immediately* say they do not want to go to school (the "thinking" part). Then they work themselves up, become very upset, and develop aches and pains as a result (the "feelings" part). At this point, they may cry, hide, throw a temper tantrum, or have trouble getting on the school bus (the "doing" part).

Other children begin with certain behaviors first (figure 3.4). For example, a girl I once worked with (I'll call her Hailey) woke up in the morning and immediately began to cry and say that she did not want to go to school. Then on the way to school she would have problems with diarrhea. In Hailey's case, the "doing" part of distress started first (crying), followed by

Figure 3.2
Distress diagram (stomachache)

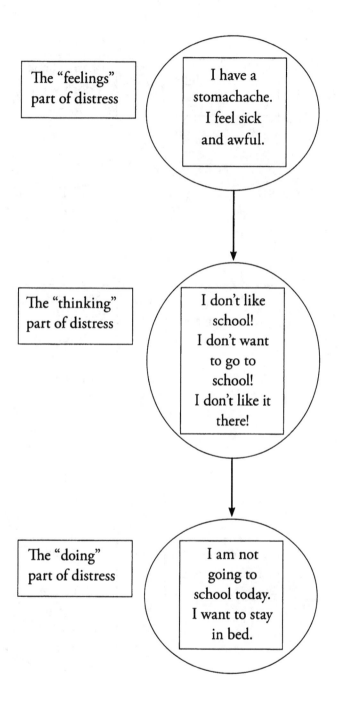

Figure 3.3
Distress diagram (school)

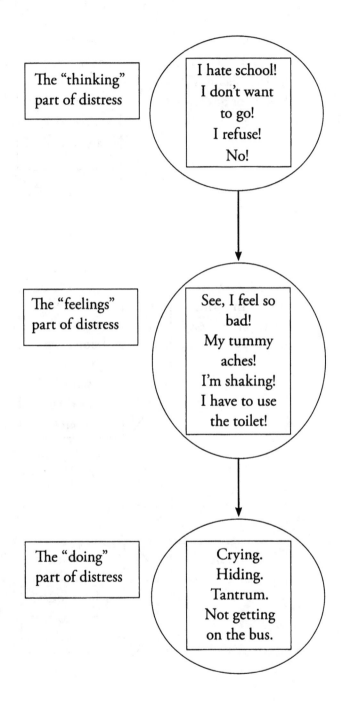

The "thinking"
part of distress

I hate school!
I don't want
to go!
I refuse!
No!

The "feelings"
part of distress

See, I feel so
bad!
My tummy
aches!
I'm shaking!
I have to use
the toilet!

The "doing"
part of distress

Crying.
Hiding.
Tantrum.
Not getting
on the bus.

Figure 3.4
Distress diagram (crying)

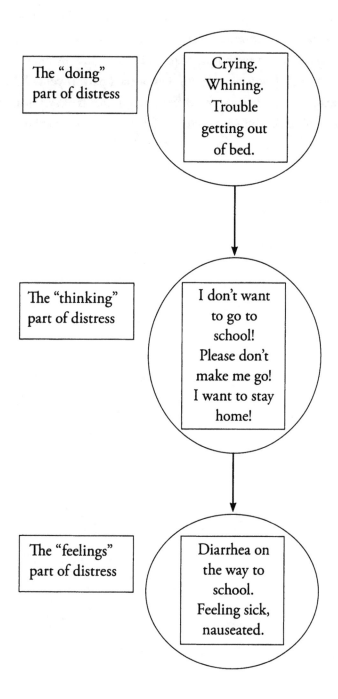

The "doing" part of distress

Crying. Whining. Trouble getting out of bed.

The "thinking" part of distress

I don't want to go to school! Please don't make me go! I want to stay home!

The "feelings" part of distress

Diarrhea on the way to school. Feeling sick, nauseated.

the "thinking" part (saying she did not want to go to school), followed by the "feelings" part (diarrhea).

What pattern of distress seems to best fit your child? In the space below, draw the most common pattern of distress that you see in your child. Feel free to follow the examples just given in the figures by drawing circles and arrows and by writing a description of each part. If your child shows different patterns of distress on different days, that is okay. Go ahead and list below all of the different patterns of distress that your child shows.

Now that you have mapped out your child's patterns of distress, see whether you listed any physical "feelings" that your child may have. If your child has *no* physical feelings of distress, then this section will be less helpful to you (you can skip ahead to the "thinking" and "doing" sections). However, if your child has some physical feelings of distress, then this section will be more helpful to you.

A reminder: Be sure that any physical feelings or symptoms your child may have are not caused by a real medical condition. The methods in this chapter will be less helpful if your child's symptoms are caused by some illness or other medical condition. If you are unsure, then schedule an appointment with your family pediatrician as soon as possible for a medical evaluation.

There are different methods of helping your child lower physical "feelings" of distress and relax more. A child cannot be physically tense and relaxed at the same time, so we want to make sure that your child is relaxed instead of tense. I am going to discuss three main approaches for lowering distress and increasing relaxation: breathing, muscle relaxation, and general relaxation. Different children respond differently to each approach, so I encourage you to try each of these to see which one your child likes most.

Breathing

The first method for lowering physical "feelings" of distress is to help your child breathe correctly. Shortness of breath or breathing too quickly (hyperventilation) can lead to a lot of distress or can be the result of feeling upset. Some children when distressed, for example, tend to take shallow breaths or take in only small puffs of air.

To correct this, ask your child to first sit in a comfortable position. Then ask your child to practice breathing in slowly through the nose (with mouth closed) and breathing out slowly through the mouth. As your child breathes in, encourage him to breathe deeply into the diaphragm (between the abdomen and chest) or stomach area, just below the rib cage. To help this along, ask your child to gently push two fingers into the diaphragm/ stomach area to feel the sensation of a full, deep breath (your child's other hand may lie on his or her chest). Try to get your child to bring in his stomach when breathing in. Then ask your child to slowly breathe out through the mouth. I recommend that you practice this breathing method with your child so that he can watch how it is done, and you can both learn to relax!

For younger children, creating some image during this process is very helpful. For example, your child may pretend that he is blowing up a tire or is a large, floating balloon. As your child breathes in, he can imagine filling up with fuel and energy. As your child breathes out, he can imagine losing fuel or energy (or tension). The idea here is to control breathing and to help your child understand the difference between feeling tense (after breathing in) and feeling more relaxed (after breathing out). If you like, you can use the following script with *your child:*

> Pretend that you are a hot-air balloon. When you breathe in, you are filling the balloon with air so that it can go anywhere you want. Breathe in through your nose like this [show for your child]. Breathe slowly and deeply—try to breathe in a lot of air! Now breathe out slowly through your mouth like air leaving a balloon. Count slowly in your head as you breathe out . . . 1 . . . 2 . . . 3 . . . 4 . . . 5. Let's try this again (practice at least three times). (Adapted from Kearney & Albano, 2007)

This breathing method is the quickest and easiest method for helping your child relax and control physical "feelings" of distress. In addition, the method can be used at any time, such as when your child is distressed. Even better, the breathing method is one that can be done without drawing a lot of attention from other people.

> *Ask your child to practice the breathing method at least three times per day for about 5 minutes each time.*

Ask your child to practice the breathing method at least three times per day for about 5 minutes each time. In addition, ask your child to practice this method in the morning before school or during the day at school as he feels distressed. If your child is mostly distressed in the evening before school, then ask him to practice this method at that time. Do not force your child to practice this method, however, if he does not want to. The breathing method will work best if your child is truly motivated to do it.

Muscle Relaxation

The second method for lowering physical "feelings" of distress is muscle relaxation. When children are distressed about school, they often feel very tense in their muscles, especially muscles surrounding the hands, face, jaw, and stomach. One way of helping your child ease muscle tension is to tense and then release different muscle groups. Try this now: Take your hand and ball it into a fist. Squeeze as hard as possible. Even harder. Hold your tense fist in place for about 10 seconds, then quickly let go. Repeat this once.

How does your hand feel? Many people say their hand feels warm, a bit tingly, and a bit more relaxed. When we tense, hold, and quickly release our muscles, the muscles usually feel looser. This method can be done with other muscle groups as well. For example:

- Bring your shoulders tightly up to your ears, hold them there for 10 seconds, and then release them quickly. Repeat this once.

- Scrunch up your face tightly, hold the tension for 10 seconds, and then release quickly. Repeat this once.

- Bite down hard with your teeth so that your jaw is firmly clenched, hold the clench for 10 seconds, and then release your jaw quickly. Repeat this once.

- Bring in your stomach tightly against your backbone, hold the tension for 10 seconds, and then release your stomach quickly. Repeat this once.

- Tense your legs or push your feet hard onto the floor, keep them tense for 10 seconds, and then release them quickly. Repeat this once.

I recommend that you try this method with your child. During a peaceful time of day, such as in the evening, ask your child to sit in a comfortable chair while you gradually guide him through different areas of muscle tension and release. Concentrate on the hands, shoulders, face, jaw, stomach, and legs/feet. This process should go *slowly*. Praise your child as he completes each step. If you like, you can use the following script with *your child:*

(Speaking slowly and in a low voice) Okay, sit down, try to relax, and close your eyes. Try to make your body droopy and floppy, like you are a wet towel. Take your right hand and squeeze it as hard as you can. Hold it tight! (Wait 5 to 10 seconds.) Now let go quickly. Good job. Let's do that again. Take your right hand and squeeze it as hard as you can. Hold it. (Wait 5 to 10 seconds.) Now let go quickly. See how that feels. Nice and warm and loose. Now take your left hand and squeeze it as hard as you can. Hold it tight! (Wait 5 to 10 seconds) Now let go quickly. Good job. Let's do that again. Take your left hand and squeeze it as hard as you can. Hold it. (Wait 5 to 10 seconds.) Now let go quickly. See how that feels. Nice and warm and loose.

Now shrug your shoulders hard and push them up to your ears. Make your shoulders really tight. Hold them there. (Wait 5 to 10 seconds.) Now let go quickly. Great. Let's do that again. Shrug your shoulders hard and push them up to your ears. Make your shoulders really tight. Hold them there. (Wait 5 to 10 seconds.) Now let go quickly. Great job.

Now scrunch up your face as much as you can. Make your face seem really small and tight. Now hold it there. (Wait 5 to 10 seconds.) Now let your face go droopy. Good. Let's do that again. Scrunch up your face as much as you can. Make your face seem really small and tight. Now hold it there. (Wait 5 to 10 seconds.) Now let your face go droopy. Good job.

Now I want you to bite down real hard with your teeth. Make your jaw really tight. Hold it there. (Wait 5 to 10 seconds.) Now open your jaw. How does that feel? Good. Let's try that again. Bite down real hard with your teeth. Make your jaw really tight. Hold it there. (Wait 5 to 10 seconds.) Now open your jaw. Try to make it as loose as you can. Good practicing!

Let's go to your stomach now. Bring in your stomach as much as you can —make it real tight! Press it against your backbone. Now hold it there. (Wait 5 to 10 seconds.) Now let go quickly. That feels better. Let's try that again. Bring in your stomach as much as you can—make it real tight! Press it against your backbone. Now hold it there. (Wait 5 to 10 seconds.) Now let go quickly. Great job.

Okay, one more. Push your feet onto the floor real hard so your legs feel really tight. Push hard! Now hold it. (Wait 5 to 10 seconds.) Now relax your legs. Shake them a little. Let's try that again. Push your feet onto the floor real hard so your legs feel really tight. Push hard! Now hold it. (Wait 5 to 10 seconds.) Now relax your legs. Shake them a little. Good practicing!

Now try to make your whole body really droopy: pretend you are a wet towel! Relax your whole body and see how nice that feels. You did a great job relaxing. Okay, open your eyes. (Adapted from Ollendick & Cerny, 1981)

Practice this script *at least once a day* with your child, preferably in the evening. If you don't have time for the whole script, then concentrate on whatever area of your child's body seems most tense. In Caleb's case, for example, his mother concentrated on her son's stomach area, asking him to tense and release his muscles there so he felt looser. He later practiced this method during the school day whenever he felt uncomfortable.

As your child becomes better able to relax independently, have him practice the entire script at least twice per day. In addition, ask your child to practice this method in the morning before school when he feels most tense. Be sure to praise your child for practicing muscle relaxation.

General Relaxation

The third method for lowering physical "feelings" of distress involves breathing and relaxation tapes and feedback from you. Many breathing, relaxation, and yoga tapes are available on the market. Some of these involve relaxing sounds such as ocean waves and others involve special instructions about how to breathe properly and relax. Because different children respond differently to various methods, I encourage you to do some research and discuss with your child which type of breathing or relaxation tape might be best for him. If you or your child do not like this idea, that is fine; your child can use the breathing or muscle relaxation methods just described.

Another important piece of relaxation is feedback from you. Whenever you notice that your child is particularly tense, gently encourage him to practice one or more of the relaxation methods described here. Do not insist upon this or force your child to do these methods, however. The methods will work best if your child chooses to do them on his own or with your help. If your child absolutely refuses to practice these methods, then feel free to rely more on the other methods discussed in this chapter.

If your child is distressed for much of the school day, ask your child's teacher to rate your child's level of distress and to encourage your child to use the methods described here. I generally do not recommend that you or your spouse/partner call your child during the day or ask that he contact you. The best result is a situation where your child can control his or her physical "feelings" of distress independently. As your child does so, be sure that you and your child's teacher give a lot of praise.

Changing the "Thinking" Part of Distress

As I mentioned earlier, younger children such as Caleb often do not have detailed thoughts about their distress. Instead, they tend to say things such as, "I don't like school" or "I feel bad when I'm at school." So you might be wondering: What do I do when my child says these things?

First, do not use statements such as, "Don't worry," "Snap out of it," "There's nothing to be afraid of," "You're not really upset," or "You're faking it." These statements do not work to improve school attendance and can actually make matters worse. For example, if a boy is distressed about school and a parent tells him not to worry, he will feel even worse when he continues to worry. Or a child may feel that his parents do not believe his statements about being in distress. Remember that your child is truly distressed about school, whatever the reason may be.

Second, do not *constantly* reassure your child. For example, do not say over and over, "It will be okay" or "You'll be fine" when he is crying or

Home Schooling

Children who do not want to go to school often ask their parents to enroll them in home schooling. Home schooling refers to a situation where a child is taught at home by a parent, tutor, or some other adult who usually follows some school-based curriculum. Traditionally, home schooling was reserved for children with severe medical or other problems that did not allow them to attend regular school. In recent times, however, more parents have switched to home-based methods of education.

Is home schooling right for you and your child? Certainly the benefits of home schooling include good supervision of the child, increased parent-child contact, and better control over what a child learns. On the flip side, however, withdrawing a child from school tends to isolate him or her from social gatherings and peer groups where he or she can build social skills, learn to perform well before others, and develop friendships. In addition, the quality of a child's education at home versus school must be considered.

Home schooling is generally not a good idea for dealing with a child who is distressed about school. If your child is trying to avoid such distress, then giving in to this behavior by enrolling him or her in home schooling only rewards or reinforces avoidance. In other words, your child may be even more likely to avoid other situations in the future. A better method of dealing with school refusal behavior in particular and avoidance in general is to practice the skills for managing distress that I cover in this chapter and in chapter 4. These skills include learning to relax, thinking more realistically, and gradually facing whatever situation is causing the distress. As children learn to lower their distress, school will, we hope, become a more enjoyable place to be.

upset. Saying these things once is fine, but saying them over and over only rewards your child's statements about not wanting to go to school. I know it is human nature to want to reassure your child and let him know that everything will be okay. But do this just once. The rest of the time try to focus on getting ready for school (see chapter 5), tell your child to practice correct breathing or relaxing, and remind him what needs to be done, such as finishing breakfast. Speak to your child in a neutral and matter-of-fact tone that suggests that going to school is normal and expected.

Third, do not promise your child extra things for going to school. Some children suddenly become less distressed when their parents promise to buy them a toy or let them stay up later that night in exchange for going to school. *Do not fall into this trap!* Instead, tell your child that you expect him to go to school and that he can discuss his feelings with you that night. For now, though, everyone has to go to work and school.

Finally, please watch your own behavior carefully. Many distressed children also have distressed parents. Feeling nervous yourself is okay except when your child copies the nervousness or copies poor ways of handling nervousness. For example, some children copy their parents' physical feelings, thoughts, and behaviors of distress. In addition, children watch how their parents cope with distress and pay close attention to their parents' statements of distress or avoidance of situations. If this applies to you, try to set a good example for your child. This means practicing methods of relaxation with your child, refraining from obvious statements about distress, and working hard in the morning to get ready for school or work. In addition, have others praise you and your child for being brave and for tackling the day ahead!

Changing the "Doing" Part of Distress

If your child is distressed about school but goes to school every day, then concentrate on the "feelings" and "thinking" parts of distress that we have covered in this chapter. However, if your child is distressed about school *and* is missing school, then you must also concentrate on the "doing" part of distress, which involves your child's avoidance and absenteeism. The "doing" part of distress is what I will focus on for the rest of this chapter.

Please note that the methods we are about to cover will require (1) a lot of work on your part and (2) support from other people. If you and your spouse/partner work full-time, for example, then you will need to make some arrangement at work to accommodate the part-time school schedules we are about to discuss. Or you will need to arrange some form of supervised child care during the day. Perhaps you have already done this because your child is missing school. If not, then be sure to make these arrangements as soon as possible. Consider extended family members such as grandparents or other relatives as well as friends, neighbors, church members, and others who can help you during this process.

When Should I Keep My Child Home From School?

Parents often ask me which physical "feelings" should keep their child home from school. In general, I recommend that a child go to school *except* when there is:

- A temperature of 100 degrees or more

- Frequent vomiting

- Bleeding

- Lice

- Severe diarrhea

- Severe flu-like symptoms

- Another very severe medical condition such as intense pain

If your child has these problems, seek the advice of your pediatrician. In addition, I recommend that a child with these problems remain in bed throughout the school day or complete schoolwork at home. Do not allow your child to do many fun things during the school day because this only rewards him for not being in school. If your child is too sick to go to school, he is too sick to play! If your child is absent from school for more than a couple of days because of these problems, contact your child's teacher(s) to arrange for homework that she can complete during the day.

Other than for some severe medical problem, I recommend that your child go to school. Minor headaches, stomachaches, or nausea are not enough to keep a child home and might be managed by over-the-counter medication (talk to your pediatrician). If your child's symptoms become more severe during the school day, then he or she can visit the nurse's office. *You will have more success getting your child to go to school if you expect and encourage school attendance every day.* Only extreme circumstances, and not more minor ones such as a cold, should keep a child home from school, especially a child with a history of school refusal behavior.

If your child is missing school, then he is likely to be (1) coming in late to school in the mornings or (2) missing most of the school day altogether. I will discuss each of these problems separately. If your child is coming in late in the mornings, it may be because he is having problems leaving the house or entering the school building. Let's talk about this problem first.

Coming in Late in the Morning

Many parents say their child is most distressed just as he has to enter the school building. Their child may get ready for school with little problem, ride in the car on the way to school, walk to the playground with Mom or Dad, and the crying starts and he will not go into school. Such was the case for Caleb.

What then? Your first step in this situation should be to inform school officials about what is going on (if they don't already know). Contact your child's guidance counselor, for example, to let him or her know that your child has trouble entering the school building. In addition, tell the guidance counselor that your child may be late to school but that you will be trying hard to make sure that your child goes to school for at least part of the school day. The guidance counselor may also help the situation by greeting your child at a certain time and place in the morning and by escorting your child to class (if possible). If your child is willing to be escorted into the classroom by a school official, then allow this to happen and leave quickly.

If you can get your child to school but not in the school building, *do not go immediately home with your child!* Going immediately home with your child only reinforces crying and avoidance of school (like canceling the dentist appointment). Instead, stay at the school playground or entrance or sit in your car in the parking lot with your child. Encourage your child to use the methods described earlier to breathe correctly and to relax muscles.

Do not get angry or criticize your child (it's understandable that you may be irritable). Also, do not say statements such as, "Don't worry," "Snap out of it," "There's nothing to be afraid of," "You're not really upset," or "You're faking it." Instead, remain calm and speak to your child in a matter-of-fact tone. Let your child vent whatever it is that he is concerned about, but tell your child that he is expected to go to school. If you have to sit or stand in silence, that is fine. Encourage your child every 15 minutes or so to enter the school building. Even if this goes on for a couple of hours and your child then goes into school, this is better than having your child miss the entire school day. If your child is missing more than a couple of hours of school, then read the next section.

A key rule here is no backsliding! This means that you should not let your child do less than what he has shown he can already do. For example:

- If your son can make it to the entrance or main lobby of the school building, then wait with him there as long as possible and encourage him to go in every 15 minutes or so. Again, if your child is eventually willing to go to class with a school official, then let this happen and leave quickly.

- If your daughter can make it to a supervised setting such as the guidance counselor's office or school library, then escort her there and have her remain there for some time before entering class. If possible, leave the school building and allow your child to be escorted to class by a school official.

- If your son can make it into the classroom after some period of time, even if he is late, then allow him to do so (then read the next section).

If your child is having problems getting ready for school in the morning, see chapter 5 for recommendations on structuring the morning routine. If your child is missing most of the school day, then read the next section.

Missing Most of the School Day

If your child is distressed about school and is missing most of the school day, then we must arrange a gradual schedule of returning him to school. Because your child may be overwhelmed now by the entire school day, and because we want your child to practice the methods described earlier in this chapter, a part-time schedule of attendance may be what we have to shoot for first. There are different ways of doing this, and I will cover each one. Of course, the eventual goal of this approach is to ease your child toward full-time attendance with little distress.

Before starting a part-time attendance schedule, *you must meet with relevant school officials* to plot a course that is acceptable to both you and them. Key school officials would be your child's guidance counselor, school psychologist, or principal (you should have their contact information written down in chapter 1). Find out who you need to visit to put a part-time schedule plan in motion. In addition, explain to this person why you are doing so:

to gradually get your child more used to school while working to lower his physical feelings of distress.

Adding One Step at a Time

If your child is missing most of the school day, then the first step toward full-time school attendance should be small. Ask your child what time of day is easiest for him to go to school. Some kids say that school would be great if only they could leave at lunchtime. Other kids say that school would be great if they had to go only in the afternoon. Still other kids say they like only lunchtime or maybe a couple of classes such as science and band. Once you know what time of day your child is most likely to go to school, then you know where to start.

The first step in a part-time schedule can involve one of the following:

- Your child goes to school in the morning and is then allowed to come home within an hour (then you gradually work forward by adding more time).

- Your child goes to school at 2 p.m. and is then allowed to come home when school normally ends, say at 3:10 p.m. (then you gradually work backward by adding more time).

- Your child goes to school only for lunch and is then allowed to come home afterward (then you gradually add more school time before and after lunch).

- Your child goes to school only for his favorite class or time of day (then you gradually add more classes or school time).

- Your child attends a schoolroom other than his classroom, such as the school library, guidance counselor or nurse's office, or main lobby (then you gradually add more classroom time).

Let's discuss each of these approaches separately. *As you try one of these approaches, be sure to keep track of your child's daily attendance by using the worksheet provided in chapter 2.* Doing this will allow you to see if what you are doing is indeed working and if another approach is needed. Try not to switch your approach unless you have tried it for at least 1 week and preferably 2 weeks. If one approach is not working after a couple of weeks, then a different one may be tried. Be sure to consult with your child's guidance counselor or other school officials during this process. Also, always let your child know in advance what the plan is for the next school day.

Morning

Younger children usually respond best to a part-time schedule that involves some morning classroom time before they are allowed to come home. If you decide to choose this option, then tell your child that he is expected to go to school and that you (or someone) will pick him or her up at 10 a.m. (then be sure to do this!). If your child does go to school with little fuss under this condition, then be sure to give a lot of praise. When your child is home the rest of the day, require him to complete schoolwork that you can collect from your child's teacher. If your child has completed all of his schoolwork or none was sent home, then require that he continue to do academic tasks such as read books, practice multiplication tables, or tackle educational games on the computer.

Do not let your child do fun things during regular school hours. If your child did go to school as planned (even if for the hour) *and* completed academic tasks during the day, then he can be allowed to play or do other fun things *after* school hours. If your child did not go to school as planned or did not complete academic tasks during the day, then he should be grounded and not allowed fun activities that day. Instead, ask your child to work around the house, send him to bed early, and say that you expect better behavior the next day (for more detailed information about rewards and punishments, see chapter 5).

Be sure to track your child's level of distress each day (see chapter 2). Once your child's level of distress is low when attending school for an hour, another hour can be added. How do you know if distress has been lowered enough? I recommend that the distress level at each step at least be cut in half. So, if your rating of your child's distress averages about an "8" every day, then wait until the distress level is "4" or less before going on to the next step. If your child still seems quite distressed after some period of time, say more than a week, then perhaps the time that he is in school is too long. If so, reduce it a bit, perhaps to 30 minutes, *but still require your child to go to school.*

If your child's distress level becomes low rather quickly, which sometimes happens, then go to the next step. The next step can be adding another hour to the school day—in this case, for example, you may be picking your child up from school at 11 a.m. instead of 10 a.m. The rest of the day should then go as discussed above. Once your child has mastered this step, add an hour at a time until he can go to school for the entire day. Be sure to keep rating his level of distress and talk to your child and his teacher(s) to be sure that distress has been truly lowered.

If your child misses the hour of school that was scheduled, keep trying during the school day to get that hour of attendance (see previous section). If necessary, sit with your child at school or in the car at school and encourage him every 15 minutes or so to enter the school building. Be sure that your child practices the methods described earlier for lowering physical feelings of distress. *Remember: no backsliding!* If your child has shown that he can go to school for at least 2 hours, for example, then this is the minimum amount of school that he should attend.

Afternoon

Other children prefer to go to school in the afternoon and gradually add more time to school by working backward. For example, a child may be expected to go to school at 2 p.m. and then be allowed to come home as school normally ends, say at 3:10 p.m. In this case, the same gradual process of adding school applies. Once a child can go to school from 2 to 3:10 p.m. with little distress, for example, then an hour can be added (so, 1 to 3:10 p.m.). This is continued until full-time school attendance is reached. During the day up to formal school attendance, your child should be completing schoolwork or other academic tasks.

The downside of using this schedule, as you might imagine, is that it leaves little room for error. If your child absolutely refuses to go to school at 2 p.m., then there is little time left to salvage at least some school attendance (unlike in the morning, where you can keep trying for a whole day to get at least some attendance). Therefore, consider this option very carefully and perhaps as a last resort. This option is probably best for children whose parents are very confident that they will follow through with instructions to go to school in the afternoon.

My Child Won't Ride the School Bus!

Many children who are distressed about school do miss school, but others simply have problems riding the school bus. If your child has problems riding the school bus, it may be due to worry about becoming sick or getting closer to school. In other cases, though, children cannot say why they get distressed on the school bus—they just do!

If your child has this problem, then ask him to take just a short trip on the school bus. This may involve simply standing at the school bus stop, getting on the bus, and then stepping off before you drive him to school. Or, your child may get on the school bus and ride it to a next stop that may be just a minute or so away. As your child does this, be sure that he practices the methods of lowering distress that I cover in this chapter. In addition, rate your child's level of distress during each step (using the worksheet given in chapter 2).

As your child masters these early steps, gradually increase the length of time that she rides the bus. This may involve riding for a longer period of time or arriving at more stops, for example (perhaps add one stop every few days or so). Praise your child for doing each step successfully. Try to get to the point where your child can ride the bus all the way to school with you driving behind the bus.

At this point, work backward. When your child is 5 minutes away from school, for example, drive away and let her finish alone (you can tell your child in advance about this). Once he she can handle this, then gradually increase the amount of time that he she is riding without you following behind. Give your child a lot of praise when she can finally make it there alone!

Lunch

Another part-time school attendance option is to start at lunchtime and work from the middle of the day outward. In this case, require your child to eat lunch with his classmates, which is often an enjoyable and less distressing time for youngsters. The advantage of this approach is that the child is being exposed to at least some part of the school day and will likely interact with peers, who will encourage your child to go to class. If you choose this option, then your child is first expected to attend lunch only. He can complete schoolwork or other academic tasks during the morning and afternoon at home.

Once your child can eat lunch at school with ease, gradually increase classroom time just before and just after lunch. A good place to start is 30 minutes before lunch and 30 minutes after lunch. So, if your child has lunch from noon to 12:45 p.m., require that he be in the classroom from 11:30 a.m. to noon and from 12:45 to 1:15 p.m. As your child is better able to handle this schedule, gradually increase the amount of time in class until full-time attendance is reached.

Favorite Time of Day

Some kids tell me they would be willing to go to school if they had to go only to science class. So, I tell them: go to science class! *Attending school for at least one class or for at least part of the school day is far, far better than no attendance at all.* If your child is in this category, then require him to go to the classes that he likes best. Once your child is attending this class regularly with little distress, then his second-favorite class can be added. Once your child is attending these two classes regularly with little distress, then his third-favorite class can be added, and so forth. *Remember: no backsliding!* Once your child has shown that he can attend a certain number of classes, then this is the minimum amount of time he should be in school each day.

Some parents ask me at this point whether switching a child's classes is a good idea. If the "switching around" involves just a class or two, this is usually not a problem. But, if your child wants his entire schedule changed, he may be delaying the process of going back to school. Work with your child's guidance counselor to "tweak" your child's schedule if necessary, but make it clear to your child that he is expected to attend school full-time eventually and no matter the schedule.

Attending School But Outside the Classroom

Other kids have told me over the years that the problem is not being in the school building but being in their classroom. If your child matches this situation, then arrange with school officials so that he attends school in some supervised setting outside the classroom. Your child may, for example, spend the day in the school library doing schoolwork or helping the librarian restock the shelves. Or he may sit in the main office or counselor's or nurse's office all day. Each of these scenarios is much better than sitting home all day.

As your child becomes more used to being in the school building, and becomes more relaxed and less distressed, gradually increase the amount of time that he spends in the classroom. This may involve small steps such as an hour at a time or larger steps such as a whole morning or afternoon (whatever your child can handle at that time). If your child is very resistant to going into the class, arrange to have a couple of his classmates (or the entire class) visit your child and encourage him to come to class. The

Those Sunday Evening Blues

When children finally go back to school, some are still a little distressed on Sunday evenings before the start of the school week. This is normal for many kids, but distress may be especially tough on your child. If your child is distressed in the evenings before school, particularly on Sunday evening, then be sure to talk to him about his concerns. Be supportive, but make it clear that he is expected to go to school the next day. Ask your child to practice the breathing and relaxation methods described in this chapter if they are helpful. In addition, if your child is focused on the entire school week, then encourage him to focus on going to school just one day at a time. After all, your child's teacher can't cram a whole week of school into Monday!

Some parents plan a whole bunch of activities on Sunday night to distract children from thinking about school. Trust me, though: your child will still think about school, and that's okay. A better idea is to plan a fun family get-together on Sunday afternoon but allow your child to rest comfortably Sunday evening. Planning something small but special on Monday evening is also a good idea so your child has something to look forward to. Examples include getting to stay up 20 minutes later for going to school on time that morning, enjoying a favorite dessert, or playing a game with Mom.

As you talk to your child during the week, be sure to praise even minor things such as entering the school building, crying less, and being brave. In addition, you can point out to your child how going to school helps Mom and Dad. Knowing that you appreciate your child's effort will go a long way toward making the morning seem less dreadful and will help motivate her to keep going to school.

classmates can, for example, say what fun things they are doing or that they miss your child. Obviously these suggestions require a lot of cooperation from school officials, so make sure everyone is "on board" before beginning.

Do's and Don'ts!

I know that I have given you a lot of information in this chapter. Here is a list of some do and don't reminders:

Do:

- Help your child understand the different parts of distress: the physical "feelings," "thinking," and "doing" parts of distress.

- Think about how these different parts of distress occur in your child.

- Teach your child correct breathing by using deep, slow, diaphragmatic breathing.

- Teach your child to relax his muscles using the tense-and-release method.

- Encourage your child to relax in general and give him feedback about doing so.

- Speak to your child in a calm, matter-of-fact tone.

- Expect your child to go to school each day.

- Work closely with school officials when developing your morning plan.

- Wait at school with your child as long as possible.

- Set up a part-time school attendance schedule if necessary.

- Seek support from others.

- Be consistent and use these methods every day.

Don't:

- Fight, yell, lecture, criticize, negotiate, beg, or bribe your child to go to school.

- Ignore your child's distress.

- Use statements such as "Don't worry," "Snap out of it," "There's nothing to be afraid of," "You're not really upset," or "You're faking it."

- Linger at school or the playground when your child goes to class.

- Allow your child to come home early or do fun things during school hours.

Final Comments

Having a child who is distressed about school and who is missing school can be very upsetting, but the problem is fixable! Lowering a child's distress and getting him back into school is best accomplished with a lot of persistence, patience, structure, support from others in your life, and cooperation with school officials who can help. You can do it!

Children Who Refuse School to Avoid Social and Performance Situations

Raven is a 13-year-old girl who has problems attending school because she is nervous in different social and performance situations at school. Raven has skipped several classes already this year and has three full-day absences. She says she is shy, feels uncomfortable talking to other kids at school, and does not like speaking before others or going to gym class. In particular, she has been skipping classes where she has to take tests or give oral presentations, and her teachers complain that Raven will not answer questions in class.

This chapter will be *more helpful* to you if your child matches Raven's situation or if one or both of the following is true:

- Your child is having trouble going to school or classes because of distress about social or performance situations at school.

- Your child is missing certain classes such as gym, choir, band, reading, English, or other courses where performing before others is expected.

This chapter will be *less helpful* to you if one or both of the following is true:

- Your child is not distressed about school.

- Your child is refusing school *only* for attention (see chapter 5).

- Your child is refusing school *only* to do more fun activities outside of school (see chapter 6).

▦ *Children Who Refuse School to Avoid Social and Performance Situations*

In chapter 2 we discussed different reasons why children have trouble going to school. One reason is that some children, like Raven, want to get away from distress they feel when talking to others (*social situations*) or when performing in front of others (*performance situations*). In Raven's case, for example, she was somewhat shy and had problems talking to other kids at school. In particular, she had trouble starting conversations or keeping conversations going. In addition, she did not like the spotlight to be on her, so she was nervous when she felt others were watching her do something like answer a question in class, change clothes in the locker room, or give an oral report (see chapter 2 for more examples). As a result, she sometimes avoided classes or other situations at school where these things occurred.

If you read chapter 2 or 3, you learned that many youngsters are distressed about school but cannot say what bothers them. Older children, however, like Raven, are better able to describe the distress they feel at school and what is bothering them there. In particular, older kids often say their distress about school is due to social or performance situations. Knowing about these situations is good because it gives us specific targets to shoot at, such as helping your child talk to others or give an oral presentation in class. If your child is missing school, then easing her distress in these situations will also help improve school attendance.

The main goals of this chapter are to help your child lower distress in social and performance situations and improve her school attendance. To do so, I will concentrate on the following:

- ▦ Understanding what distress is: the "feeling," "thinking," and "doing" parts of distress

- ▦ Lowering physical "feelings" of distress

- ▦ Dealing with the "thinking" part of distress, or how to help your child think more realistically in social or performance situations

- ▦ Managing the "doing" part of distress by monitoring your child's school attendance and increasing her time in the classroom.

If you read chapter 3, and I recommend you do, then you might be wondering how this chapter is different. Yes, there are some similarities between what I recommend for younger children with general distress (chapter 3) and what I recommend for older children and adolescents with social and performance distress (this chapter). But because older kids with social and performance distress often have more detailed thoughts, the "thinking" part of distress receives a lot more attention in this chapter.

Why Am I Doing This?

If your child resembles Raven, my guess is that she is pretty distressed about different social or performance situations at school. Your child may be distressed about these situations in the morning before school, during the school day, or even in the evening before the next school day. Your child may talk a lot about her distress or may be kind of quiet about it. That's okay.

To tackle your child's distress, both you and your child should understand what distress actually is. As mentioned in chapter 3, distress can sometimes seem overwhelming and uncontrollable. However, distress can actually be broken down into smaller parts that are easier to understand and control. This will be our first step. If you think this chapter applies to your older child or adolescent, then I *strongly encourage* you to involve her in reading this chapter and fully discussing its contents.

Many children who are distressed have uncomfortable physical feelings such as trembling, shaking, "butterflies in the stomach," and shortness of breath or hyperventilation (breathing too quickly). To help ease these feelings, we will concentrate on correct breathing and relaxation techniques that your child can use when upset. These exercises are quick, painless, and easy to use. Many children say they feel more comfortable when they have a way of controlling these distressing feelings.

A main focus of this chapter, however, will be to change the way your child thinks about different social or performance situations. Many older children and adolescents wrongly believe that terrible, horrible things will happen in different social and performance situations. As a result, they avoid these situations and miss school. So, one focus of this chapter will be to help you help your child think more realistically in these situations.

Another major focus of this chapter will be to gradually increase the amount of time your child participates in social and performance situations at school. As your child becomes more comfortable and confident in these situations, her school attendance is also likely to improve. Remember that the main goals of this chapter are to help your child be more comfortable about going to school and to stay in school for the entire day. Let's talk next about what distress actually is.

What Is Distress?

You may recall from chapter 2 that "distress" can refer to your child's level of anxiety, worry, uneasiness, discomfort, nervousness, apprehensiveness, or dread about school. Distress in children is shown in different ways, but among older children and adolescents this often includes avoidance, withdrawal, sadness, noncompliance, irritability, restlessness, and verbal statements asking to stay home, among other ways. Your child may also have a unique way of showing her distress, and you should keep this in mind as we go along.

Distress or anxiety is made up of *three main parts*:

- A "feelings" part that involves uncomfortable physical problems such as trembling, shaking, "butterflies in the stomach," and shortness of breath or hyperventilation (breathing too quickly)

- A "thinking" part that involves uncomfortable thoughts or worries about bad things happening, such as worrying that everyone will laugh as a child changes clothes in a locker room or that the child will stutter badly during an oral presentation at school

- A "doing" part that usually involves moving away from something that causes distress, such as avoiding school or withdrawing from people at a social gathering

Do these parts look familiar to you or your child? Let's talk about each one in more detail.

The "Feelings" Part of Distress

My guess is that your child is nervous about social or performance situations at school and that she is quite upset when in school. When older children and adolescents are distressed about speaking to others or performing in front of others, they often have uncomfortable physical feelings such as trembling, shaking, muscle tension, or breathing problems.

As I mentioned in chapter 3, feeling uncomfortable in certain situations is common and affects everyone. An important thing for you and your child to remember is that everyone gets distressed from time to time—that's part of being human! I encourage you to talk to your child about situations that make different people in your lives nervous or distressed. Think, for example, about how Mom may not like to confront a mechanic about getting a car fixed, how Dad may not like to ask people for directions, and how Uncle Joe doesn't like to go to parties or wedding receptions (yes, I know, I'm being a little stereotypical here). The point is that everyone feels uncomfortable in different situations from time to time, and your child is no different.

Most people who are distressed in certain situations, however, are able to control their distress and move forward with what they have to do. For example, Uncle Joe may understand that Aunt Jo really wants him to go to the wedding reception, so he "puts aside" his nervousness and goes. Other people, however, including your child at this point, have trouble controlling their distress in these situations. Therefore, we have to teach your child ways to control uncomfortable feelings and to move forward toward full-time school attendance.

A reminder: If your child is distressed about some legitimate threat at school, the methods in this chapter will be less helpful to you. If she is distressed about the possibility of being attacked or bullied, for example, *then this threat must be resolved first*. If a true threat has been removed and your child is *still* having trouble going to school, then the methods in this chapter may be more helpful.

Be sure to keep track of your child's level of distress each day by using the worksheet provided in chapter 2. If you like, you can give a rating for each part of distress: the "feelings" part, the "thinking" part, and the "doing" part. Or you can simply give one rating that involves all of these together. As you and your child practice the methods in this chapter, I will ask you to check whether the methods are working by looking at the daily distress ratings. Don't forget to record daily attendance and any morning behavior problems as well!

The "Thinking" Part of Distress

Another important part of distress is the "thinking" part. When we are distressed or anxious about something, we sometimes think about worst-case scenarios or all the terrible things that could happen to us. When we have to give a toast or speak before others, for example, we might be nervous about making a mistake, tripping over our words, or having people snicker at us. Sometimes these thoughts can be so bad that we avoid these situations.

Worrying about things is also a normal human experience; we all worry about something! But worry is not usually a problem because we understand that horrible, terrible things are not likely to happen. So even though we may be nervous about giving a toast at a party, we do it anyway because we are surrounded by family and friends who are not likely to ridicule us!

As mentioned in chapter 3, some people who are distressed focus a lot on the *worst-case scenario* and have trouble thinking about other explanations. This applies to children and adolescents as well. For example, a teenage girl might assume that others in a locker room are staring at her body and laughing, when in fact the others are joking about something else. This kind of thought is not unusual, but it can be a problem if other thoughts are "pushed away." For example, if the teenager fails to think about more reasonable explanations for what just happened, such as the possibility that others are simply laughing at a joke, then she is likely to feel quite distressed and may even skip gym class.

Think about when this happens to you. What might you think when a coworker won't speak to you one day? Might you assume that he or she is angry with you? Sure! But most people also consider other possibilities, such as the possibility that the person is having a bad day or is stressed about work and has little time for socializing.

Older children and adolescents who are distressed about social or performance situations at school tend to focus a lot on worst-case scenarios or worry that horrible, terrible things are going to happen to them. They think about all the possible things that could go wrong and how bad they will feel. In particular, they often worry about:

- Being embarrassed or humiliated before others

- Being laughed at or ridiculed in some way

- Blushing or appearing very nervous before others

Being Teased

Many kids have trouble going to school because they are teased by other kids. Teasing can be especially hurtful if directed toward sensitive areas such as weight or skin complexion. In addition, teasing can be very harmful if it is part of bullying or more serious threats. In more serious situations, be sure to consult with school officials to seek resolution of the problem.

Mild teasing is common among children, but your child may be especially sensitive to it and not want to attend school as a result. I recommend that children not respond to teasers. Although some children can deflect teasing by teasing back or by laughing it off, other kids are very bothered by teasing, so I encourage them to simply ignore any insults that are made. Do not have a child respond to provocation. Most teasers are looking for some reaction, so if they do not get a reaction they usually just move somewhere else. If your child is being teased, have her practice the breathing exercise (see chapter 3) and continue doing what she was doing before. If the teasing gets worse, advise her to walk away or seek the comfort of friends.

If this does not work, then ask your child to speak to an adult who can help at school. Although children sometimes do not like talking to adults at school about other kids, school should be a safe and comfortable place to learn. School officials are generally sensitive to these concerns, so encourage your child to speak to them as a last resort or when he feels physically threatened or when his personal space is being violated. In addition, be sure to discuss the situation with your child each evening.

- Being excluded from some social group such as a clique of friends

- Being ignored by others when speaking or asking for help

Having these thoughts or worries often leads to avoidance of school and refusal to go—this is the "doing" part of distress that I cover next.

The "Doing" Part of Distress

The final part of distress is the "doing" part, or what a child actually does when upset or worried that bad things will happen. Many older children and adolescents who are distressed about school, like Raven, "do" try to avoid school, skip classes, or withdraw from others. In most cases, worrisome thoughts and time missed from school are what bother parents the most, so I am going to concentrate on these problems later in this chapter.

As mentioned in chapter 2, avoidance of school because of social or performance distress is most common during the day at school and especially in classes where a child is expected to do something in front of others. However, many kids also avoid the entire school day if they are particularly nervous about dealing with other kids.

What does your child "feel," "think" (or say), and "do" when distressed about school? In the spaces provided below, write your child's specific feelings, thoughts (or statements), and behaviors when she is distressed about school. If your child does not have one of these parts, then go ahead and leave that part blank.

What my child "feels" when distressed

_____

_____

_____

_____

What my child "thinks" (or says) when distressed

_____

_____

_____

_____

What my child "does" when distressed

_____

_____

_____

_____

All the Parts Together

When we are distressed, we generally experience feelings and thoughts that are unpleasant. These unpleasant feelings and thoughts then lead to behaviors that cause problems. Someone who is nervous about talking to unfamiliar people at a party, for example, may start to feel physically sick or "shaky" about an hour before the party (figure 4.1). As these feelings worsen, the person may start to think about all the terrible things that could happen at the party, such as feeling isolated or hearing comments about her dress or behavior ("Why isn't she talking to anyone?"). As physical feelings and worrisome thoughts worsen, the person may be more tempted to just avoid the party (the "doing" part).

As soon as the person avoids the party and jumps on the couch to watch television, how do you suppose she feels? Much better, right? Avoiding something works well in the short-term because we feel better—the distress has been taken away! But is this a good long-term strategy? No. Sooner or later we have to interact with other people and socialize, and putting it off for a while only makes things worse. The same is true for your child's distress about school. Avoiding school might seem like a good short-term thing to do, because distress is lowered, but eventually your child has to go to school.

At this point I would like you to think about how your child's distress builds in the morning or during the course of a typical school day. What part of the distress starts first? For some older children and adolescents, the "feelings" part starts first (figure 4.2). For example, a child may wake up and feel nauseated because a big test is scheduled that day. As the stomach problem worsens, she may begin to think about terrible things that could happen as a result. For example, she may think, "What if I throw up in class today?" or "What if I'm so sick I fail my test?" As the upsetting feelings and thoughts continue, she may avoid school or skip class (the "doing" part).

Other children show other patterns of distress (figure 4.3). For example, some children wake up and *immediately* think about bad things happening: "Oh, no, a school day! I know it's going to be awful" (the "thinking" part). They may become physically unwell, very aroused, or achy as a result (the "feelings" part). At this point, they may ask their parents to allow

Figure 4.1
Distress diagram (party)

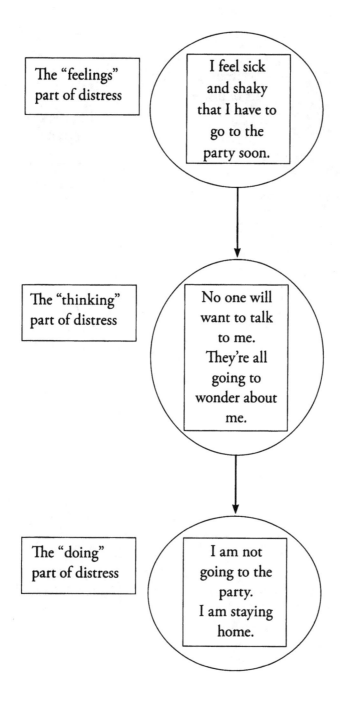

The "feelings" part of distress

I feel sick and shaky that I have to go to the party soon.

The "thinking" part of distress

No one will want to talk to me. They're all going to wonder about me.

The "doing" part of distress

I am not going to the party. I am staying home.

Figure 4.2
Distress diagram (nauseous)

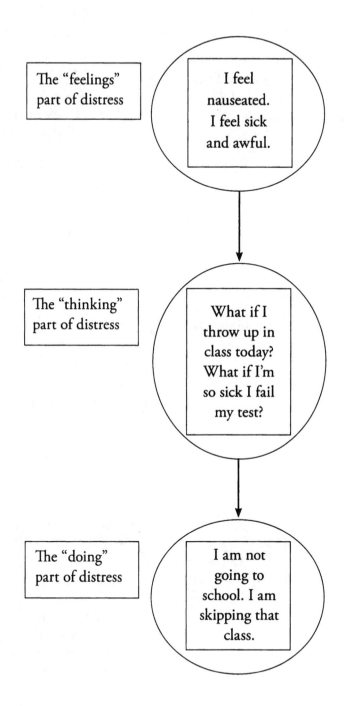

Figure 4.3
Distress diagram (bathroom)

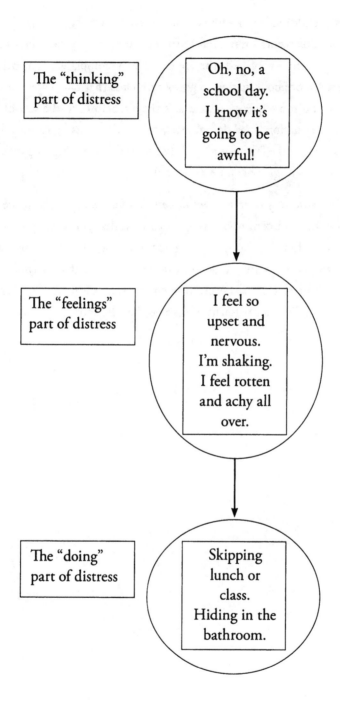

The "thinking" part of distress

Oh, no, a school day. I know it's going to be awful!

The "feelings" part of distress

I feel so upset and nervous. I'm shaking. I feel rotten and achy all over.

The "doing" part of distress

Skipping lunch or class. Hiding in the bathroom.

them to stay home, or they may skip lunch or a certain class and hide out in the bathroom (the "doing" part).

Other children begin with certain *behaviors* first (figure 4.4). For example, some adolescents simply refuse to get out of bed. When their parents try to get them out of bed, the teenagers may complain about being teased at school or about having to go to gym class that day. Later they may feel more and more queasy or dizzy as they get closer to the school building. In this situation, the "doing" part starts first (refusing to get out of bed), followed by the "thinking" part (worries about teasing or gym), followed by the "feelings" part (queasy, dizzy).

What pattern of distress seems to best fit your child? In the space provided draw the most common pattern of distress that you see in your child. Feel free to follow the examples just given in the figures by drawing circles and arrows and by writing a description of each part. If your child shows different patterns of distress on different days, that is okay. Go ahead and list all of the different patterns of distress that she shows.

Figure 4.4
Distress diagram (sleep)

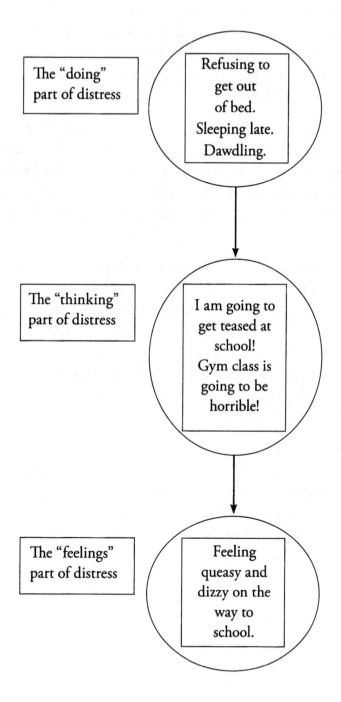

The "doing" part of distress

Refusing to get out of bed. Sleeping late. Dawdling.

The "thinking" part of distress

I am going to get teased at school! Gym class is going to be horrible!

The "feelings" part of distress

Feeling queasy and dizzy on the way to school.

Changing the "Feeling" Part of Distress

Now that you have mapped out your child's pattern of distress, see whether you listed any physical "feelings" that she may have. If your child has *no* physical feelings of distress, then this section will be less helpful to you. However, if your child has some physical feelings of distress, then this section will be more helpful to you.

A reminder: Be sure that any physical feelings or symptoms that your child may have are not caused by a real medical condition. The methods in this chapter will be less helpful if your child's symptoms are caused by some illness or other medical condition. If you are unsure, then schedule an appointment with your family pediatrician as soon as possible for a medical evaluation.

There are different methods for lowering your child's physical "feelings" of distress. Lowering "feelings" of distress is done by helping children control their arousal and relax. A child cannot be physically tense and relaxed at the same time, so we want to make sure that your child is relaxed instead of tense. Because I discussed methods of relaxation in detail in chapter 3, I invite you to read that chapter (if you have not already done so) to learn about and practice detailed methods of correct breathing, muscle relaxation, and general relaxation (see pages 71–76).

Methods of relaxation are important, but I have found over the years that many kids who are distressed about social and performance situations at school are more bothered by their *thoughts that something bad will happen in these situations*. Therefore, a main focus of this chapter will be to help you help your child change the "thinking" part of her distress. Let's talk about this next.

Changing the "Thinking" Part of Distress

If your child is distressed about social or performance situations at school, my guess is that she worries a lot about bad things happening during these situations. As I mentioned earlier, some nervousness about social and performance situations is normal because everyone gets a little uptight when meeting people for the first time, speaking in front of others, or singing or playing a musical instrument at a recital. I know that when I play the piano in front of other people, I have worries in the back of my mind about making big mistakes and not being able to finish: what would people think!

Most of us are able to set aside our worry and do what we have to do. For example, we go on a job interview to try to get a job even though we feel uncomfortable during the evaluation. Other people, though, worry so much about bad things happening that they become very upset and then avoid situations. Your child, for example, may be so worried about doing poorly in social or performance situations that she is missing school.

So, what can we do to help fix this? The main goal here is to help your child think more *realistically* in social and performance situations. Notice that I did not say "think more positively." Telling your child to "think happy thoughts," to "not worry," to "try not to think about it," or that she is a "wonderful child" will not work! If your child has worries about bad things happening at school, that is okay. But your child *must also think more realistically* about what is actually happening in situations at school.

For example, your child might worry that "everyone will laugh at me during my oral presentation." Having this thought is okay *as long as* your child takes a step back, thinks about the thought, and comes up with a more realistic thought, such as, "Some kids might laugh, but they're jerks, and most kids will just listen to me." In this situation, your child is not asked to block the negative thought or to come up with a happy thought such as "It will be okay!" *Instead*, she is asked to come up with a *more realistic thought* about what is *most likely to happen* during the oral presentation. When we think more realistically, we understand that the chance of bad things happening is actually small and we often feel less distressed.

> Changing the "thinking" part of distress is something that you and your child have to work on together.

Changing the "thinking" part of distress is something that you and your child have to work on together. In addition, for these methods to be effective:

■ You and your child *must have* a strong relationship that includes good communication.

- Your child *must be* fairly verbal, bright, and willing to discuss her worries in detail.

- In general, your child should be at least 11 years old.

- Your child *must be* doing fairly well in school or would be doing well if she were in school more.

- Your child's level of distress *must be* mild or moderate and *not* severe. Also, she should not be having panic attacks.

- Your child *must have* good social skills, such as the ability to make eye contact with others when speaking, to talk loud enough for others to hear, and to start and maintain conversations.

- Your child *must be* motivated to try to change her thoughts, practice different social and performance situations at school, and eventually go back to school.

- Your child *must not be* faced with legitimate threats or problems at school, such as bullies, intimidation, racial tension, or academic difficulties.

If any of these is not true, then you may wish to consult a qualified mental health professional (see chapter 1). This chapter will be more helpful for children who have good social skills, who should be going to school, who are not faced with real threats, but whose "thinking" part of distress prevents them from speaking to others or performing before others at school.

Negative Thoughts

What kinds of negative thoughts do older children and adolescents have in social and performance situations? In my experience, distressed youths often make the following mistakes in their thinking:

- They assume that something bad *is happening* when actually it is not. For example, a teenage girl may assume that others are laughing at her as she enters a classroom when actually the others are laughing at some inside joke.

- They assume terrible things *will happen* when terrible things are not likely to happen. For example, a teenage boy may assume that other kids will throw food at him during lunchtime when the chances of this actually happening are quite small.

- They assume what other people are thinking about them even though they cannot know. This is called "mind reading." For example, a teenage girl may assume that others believe she is ugly when she has no real knowledge of this.

- They jump to conclusions from just one event or make "mountains out of molehills" by assuming that the consequences of their acts will be extremely terrible. For example, a teenage boy may worry that he is going to fail the entire semester because of a couple of poor test marks.

- They assume they will be embarrassed and that the embarrassment will be horrible. For example, a teenage girl may assume she will sing a wrong note in choir, become embarrassed, and feel so mortified that she can never attend school again.

- They see situations as only perfect or terrible and not somewhere in between. For example, a teenage boy may assume that his school day was rotten even though some good things did happen.

- They focus much more on the negative than the positive side of things. For example, a teenage girl who performed at a recital may concentrate a lot on some wrong notes that she played instead of good overall performance of the musical piece.

- They blame themselves for things that are not within their control. For example, a teenage girl may become upset that two of her friends are fighting and blame herself for not getting more involved.

Do any of these sound familiar to you or your child? Are there other examples of thoughts that your child has in social or performance situations that make her very upset? Use the worksheet that is provided. *In the first column*, ask your child to write all social or performance situations that distress her at school. *In the second column*, ask your child to write her negative thoughts in these situations. Be sure to update these lists once a week as you work with your child. Feel free to photocopy this worksheet or download multiple copies from the companion Web site at www.oup.com/us/schoolrefusal.

Worksheet 4.1

Social/performance situations that bother me ("S")	My thoughts in this situation ("T")
_____	_____
_____	_____
_____	_____
_____	_____
_____	_____
_____	_____
_____	_____
_____	_____
_____	_____
_____	_____
_____	_____
_____	_____
_____	_____

Changing Negative Thoughts

If your child is going to school for most of the day, then schedule a discussion every evening about the negative thoughts that she had during certain social or performance situations at school that day. If your child is not going to school right now, then work toward a part-time attendance schedule (see next section on the "doing" part of distress). If your child is not going to school right now, then ask her to describe thoughts that she had in the past about social and performance situations at school. If your child cannot come up with any thoughts, then this section will be less helpful.

Once you have a pretty good idea of what thoughts or worries your child has at school, then you can start to help him or her change these thoughts. To first do so, encourage your child to use the acronym *STOP*:

- S: Am I Scared or nervous about a certain social or performance situation?

- T: What Thoughts am I having in this situation?

- O: What Other, more realistic thoughts can I have?

- P: Praise myself for thinking more realistic thoughts (adapted from Silverman & Kurtines, 1996)

Whenever your child is in a social or performance situation that causes her to be distressed, she should practice the STOP method. First, she should recognize what social and performance situations cause her the most distress; this is the "S" part of STOP. When in this social or performance situation, your child should ask herself, "Am I currently *Scared* or nervous?" If your child answers "yes" to this question, then she should think about what negative *thoughts* she is having in that situation; this is the "T" part of STOP. Ask your child to keep a written log of her thoughts in these situations so that you can discuss them together.

If your child is having negative thoughts in a social or performance situation, then she should think about *other, more realistic thoughts*; this is the "O" part of STOP. We will discuss these other thoughts in the next section. Finally, if your child was able to think more realistic thoughts in this situation, then your child should silently *praise herself* for doing so; this is the "P" part of STOP. Your child can say things such as, "Good job!," "Great thinking!," or "I am proud of myself."

Be sure to have your child practice the STOP method as much as possible whenever she is distressed in a social or performance situation at school. Your child should practice this method so often that it becomes automatic or "second nature." In other words, we want your child to practice developing more realistic thoughts in a given situation and come to realize that the chances of bad things happening are actually low and that the consequences of most situations are not that bad. Let's talk next about developing more realistic thoughts, the "O" part of STOP.

More Realistic Thoughts

If your child is having distressing thoughts in a social or performance situation at school, then be sure that she lists these thoughts for later discussion. As you and your child discuss these thoughts, *do not be judgmental or critical.* Having negative thoughts is a normal human experience; we simply have to be sure that negative thoughts are balanced and eventually replaced by more realistic thoughts. So, let's talk in more detail about how this can be done for the different negative thoughts I listed earlier.

As you and your child discuss negative thoughts, ask her to keep the following questions in mind as she challenges these thoughts:

> Am I 100% sure that this will happen (or is happening)?
>
> Can I really know what that person thinks of me?
>
> What's the worst thing that can really happen?
>
> Have I ever been in this situation before, and was it really that bad?
>
> How many times has this terrible thing actually happened?
>
> Am I the only person that has ever had to deal with this situation?
>
> So what if I'm not perfect in this situation?
>
> Is this really my fault?
>
> (adapted from Kearney & Albano, 2007)

One type of negative thought occurs when a teenager assumes that terrible things are happening when in fact they are not. For example, a teenage girl might assume that others are laughing at her as she enters a classroom when actually they are laughing at a joke. If your child has this kind of thought, encourage her to come up with more realistic thoughts by thinking about what other explanations are more likely. Be sure to use the worksheet, STOP method, and questions outlined above:

You: Okay, you wrote down that your "S" today was when you walked into class and that you thought ("T") the other kids might be laughing at you when you went into class, right?

Your child: Yeah, they were all joking around and I felt really bad.

You: Okay, so let's talk about the "O" part, some other thoughts you could have. Are you 100% sure that they were laughing at you? Be honest.

Your child: Not 100%, I guess; I don't know.

You: Okay, good. What else might have been going on?

Your child: I don't know.

You: Well, let's think about it. What else could they have been laughing at?

Your child: They're always joking around, saying dumb things. I guess they could have been doing that.

You: Great job coming up with a different thought! Yeah, you're right, maybe they were laughing at something else, because that's what they do?

Your child: Yeah, I guess that could have been happening (then praise ["P"] this new thought).

Another type of negative thought that many teenagers have is assuming that terrible things are going to happen. For example, a teenage girl who has to talk to other kids at school may assume that others will not speak to her. If your child has this kind of thought, encourage her to come up with more realistic thoughts by thinking about the worst thing that can actually happen and how many times this terrible thing has actually happened. Be sure to use the worksheet, STOP method, and questions outlined above:

You: Okay, you wrote down that your "S" today was being nervous about talking to those kids about your homework assignment and that you thought ("T") they would ignore you, right?

Your child: Yeah, I figured they would just look away.

You: Okay, so let's talk about the "O" part. What was the worst thing that could have happened if they ignored you? What would happen then? Be honest.

Your child: Well, I'd look like an idiot, I guess.

You: Okay, good. Even if the worst thing happened, and you felt kind of dumb, what could you do then?

Your child: I'd just ask somebody else.

You: Great! So, even if the worst thing happened, you could handle it, right?

Your child: Yeah, that's true.

You: And how many times have the other kids just completely ignored you?

Your child: Well, it did happen once, but usually people are nice.

You: So . . .

Your child: So I guess that the other kids won't usually ignore me, but if they do, I can just ask somebody else.

You: Great job! ("P")

Another type of negative thought that many teenagers have is assuming what other people are thinking ("mind reading"). Teenagers who are nervous in social and performance situations sometimes think they know what others are thinking and that those thoughts must be bad. For example, a teenage boy playing a musical instrument may assume that audience members think his performance is terrible, and so he becomes distressed. If your child has this kind of thought, encourage her to come up with more realistic thoughts by thinking about what other explanations are more likely and whether she really knows what others are thinking. Be sure to use the worksheet, STOP method, and questions outlined above:

You: Okay, you wrote down that your "S" today was the recital and that you thought ("T") the audience thought your performance was awful, right?

Your child: Yeah, I made some mistakes and I'm sure they thought I couldn't play.

You: Okay, so let's talk about the "O" part. Are you 100% sure that they were thinking that? Can you really know what other people are thinking about you? Be honest.

Your child: No, I was so busy reading the music I couldn't really look at the audience.

You: Okay, good. What else might they have been thinking?

Your child: I don't know, maybe that I made some mistakes?

You: Well, maybe, but you were playing in a full orchestra, right? When someone makes a mistake, can the audience really tell?

Your child: Not really. You can only tell the music is off when everybody is making a whole bunch of mistakes. Maybe they couldn't tell about me.

You: Great job coming up with a different thought! ("P") Yeah, you're right, maybe they didn't notice your mistakes because you're just one player in the orchestra?

Your child: Yeah, I guess that's right.

Another type of negative thought is when teenagers jump to conclusions from just one event or make "mountains out of molehills." They may assume that the consequences of their actions will be extremely terrible. For example, a teenage girl could assume that she is going to fail a course based on one bad test score. If your child has this kind of thought, encourage her to come up with more realistic thoughts by thinking about what other explanations are more likely and whether the consequence (failing) is really likely to happen. Be sure to use the worksheet, STOP method, and questions outlined above:

You: Okay, you wrote down that your "S" today was that you got a poor grade on your test and that you thought ("T") you would fail the whole course, right?

Your child: Yeah, I really blew that test. I can't believe it! I know I'm going to fail.

You: Okay, so let's talk about the "O" part. Are you 100% sure you will fail the whole course? What is the worst thing that can happen when you do poorly on just one test? Be honest.

Your child: Well, I might fail. . . . I don't know. Plus, there are lots of quizzes and tests this semester in that course. Plus a ton of homework and other assignments!

You: Right, so . . .

Your child: So I guess doing bad on one test won't kill me. But I can't keep doing bad!

You: Right, that's true, and we'll work on that. I'll help you. But you understand that one bad grade doesn't mean you'll fail the whole semester?

Your child: Yeah, I guess I got carried away (then praise ["P"] the new thoughts).

Another type of negative thought is when teenagers assume they will be embarrassed and that the embarrassment will be horrible. Older children and adolescents worry a lot about being embarrassed. For example, they may give an oral presentation and feel bad when tripping up their words. *The important thing to remember about embarrassment is that it is temporary and manageable!* Be sure to tell your child that everyone gets embarrassed (give some personal examples), that embarrassment doesn't usually last long, and that your child can handle the embarrassment. Be sure to use the worksheet, STOP method, and questions outlined above:

You: Okay, you wrote down that your "S" was giving your oral report and that you thought ("T") you couldn't believe you were so embarrassed, right?

Your child: Yeah, I kept tripping over my words and felt so stupid. I was *so* embarrassed!

You: Yeah, I can understand that. But let's think about the "O" part. You know, everyone gets embarrassed from time to time. Remember that time I fell off the boat and into the lake with all my clothes on at the family reunion?

Your child: (Laughing) Yeah, who could forget that!

You: I felt pretty embarrassed, but everybody gets embarrassed. Have you ever been embarrassed before?

Your child: Well, yeah, remember the time I fell off the stage during the church play?

You: Yep. And what did you do?

Your child: I just got back on stage and kept going, but I felt terrible.

You: How long did you feel terrible?

Your child: A couple of hours, I guess.

You: Right, you felt embarrassed, but it went away and you were able to handle it, right?

Your child: Yeah, I guess so.

You: So . . .

Your child: So I guess feeling embarrassed today will go away too. I already feel better now than I did at school. And I was able to finish my talk.

You: Great job! (the "P" part)

Another type of negative thought that many teenagers have is assuming that things are either perfect or terrible, and not in between. For example, a teenage girl may come home and sulk that her day was awful because of a couple of arguments with her friends. She may ignore, however, the fact that the rest of her day went well. Or a child may be upset because he did not get a perfect grade on a test. If your child has this kind of thought, encourage her to come up with more realistic thoughts by thinking about the entire day. Be sure to use the worksheet, STOP method, and questions outlined above:

You: Okay, you wrote down that your "S" was having a terrible day because of the arguments with your friends and that you thought ("T") the day was terrible, right?

My Child Is a Perfectionist!

Some children have trouble going to school because they are afraid of making mistakes! These kids may be perfectionistic—this means that they want everything to be perfect and worry a lot about the consequences of doing something wrong or handing in an assignment or worksheet that might have an error. Other perfectionists cannot complete written work because they are constantly checking and rechecking their paper. As a result, some of these kids become very distressed and may even fail their classes because nothing is being handed in! Worse yet, some refuse to go to school.

If your child is perfectionistic, then concentrate on the "thinking" part of distress. Be sure your child understands that the consequences of handing in a paper with a couple of misspellings or a test with a couple of errors are not dire—that is, a child will not fail class or be yelled at or judged harshly if a couple of mistakes are made. *In addition, be sure that you are not aggravating your child's perfectionism.* Many children who are perfectionistic have parents who are perfectionistic; as a result, children may feel a lot of pressure to do well and actually fear making mistakes. Tell your child that mistakes are normal and that you will not be angry if minor mistakes are made.

Another recommendation involves the "doing" part of perfectionism. I have often asked perfectionistic children to deliberately hand in work that has a couple of mistakes. As they do so, I tell them to practice relaxation, think realistically, and see that the consequences of the mistakes are not that bad. In addition, I stress that work needs to be handed in on time and that they must attend school. If this means a couple of minor mistakes, that is fine.

Your child: Yeah, I just feel so rotten about it. I really don't want to go back to school tomorrow.

You: It's okay to feel that way. But let's talk about the "O" part. Was every hour or 100% of the day so terrible?

Your child: Well, no, I got a great grade on my math test and had a lot of fun at lunch with Karen and Justine.

You: Great! It sounds like some of the day went well, then.

Your child: Yeah, that's true; most of the day was okay.

You: So what if your day isn't perfect, right? Is any day really perfect, where nothing bad happens?

Your child: Not really. Not in my high school, anyway.

You: My day had its ups and downs, too. Everyone's does. If a day isn't perfect, then it's a normal day!

Your child: Yeah, I guess that's right (then praise ["P"] the new thoughts).

Another type of negative thought that many teenagers have is focusing much more on the negative than the positive. For example, teenagers who are nervous about going back to school after some absence may worry a lot about the questions and comments that others may make about their absence. In addition, they may ignore the positive things that might happen. If your child has this kind of thought, encourage her to come up with more realistic thoughts by thinking about positives as well as negatives. Be sure to use the worksheet, STOP method, and questions outlined above:

You: Okay, you wrote down that your "S" is having to go back to school tomorrow and that you thought ("T") a lot of people are going to bother you with questions, right?

Your child: Yeah, everybody's going to ask me where I was and everything. I just don't want to be bothered! Can't I stay home just one more day?

You: No, you're going to school tomorrow. Let's talk about the "O" part. What else do you think everyone will say to you?

Your child: Some people will be glad I'm back. Justin called earlier and said, "See you tomorrow!"

You: Great! So you might get some looks and stares, and some people might wonder where you were, but other people will welcome you back, right?

(For more information on what children can say to others when they go back to school, see chapter 6).

Your child: Yeah, I think so. And my teachers won't say anything.

You: And do you think you'll be bothered with questions all day long?

Your child: No, probably just the morning, and I know what I can say.

You: Great! (the "P" part)

Another type of negative thought that many teenagers have is blaming themselves for things that are beyond their control. For example, a teenage girl may blame herself for conflict between two of her friends. If your child has this kind of thought, encourage her to come up with more realistic thoughts by thinking about what other explanations are more likely and whether she could really control what happened. Be sure to use the worksheet, STOP method, and questions outlined above:

You: Okay, you wrote down that your "S" was your two friends fighting and that you thought ("T") you were upset and down on yourself, right?

Your child: Yeah, they broke up and won't speak to each other. I feel so bad.

You: Why?

Your child: Because maybe I could have talked to them more.

You: Okay, let's think about the "O" part. Is this really your fault? What else might have caused them to break up?

Your child: Well, they're always fighting, and Dominic even hung out with another girl!

You: Those sound like pretty good reasons for a breakup, don't they?

Your child: Yeah, I guess so. But I still feel bad.

You: Yes, it's okay for you to feel bad for your friends, as long as you understand that sometimes people don't get along, and that's not always our fault, right?

Your child: Yeah, that's true. Maybe I can just keep being their friend (then praise ["P"] the new thoughts).

Practicing the STOP Method

If your child has a lot of negative thoughts about social and performance situations at school, then talk to her *every day* about these thoughts and help her change the thoughts to more realistic ones. In addition, have your child use the worksheet, practice the STOP method, and draw on the questions listed here to take a step back, look at negative thoughts, and come up with more realistic thoughts. With practice, your child should be able to think more realistically and discover that bad things are not likely to happen and, even if they do, that she is likely able to handle whatever does happen.

Changing the "Doing" Part of Distress

Another important goal of this chapter is changing the "doing" part of distress. Your child may either be (1) missing most of the school day or (2) having trouble going to certain classes or feeling distressed in different social or performance situations at school. Let's talk about these separately.

Missing Most of the School Day

If your child is missing most or all of the school day, then the first step toward full-time school attendance should be small. Ask your child what time of day is easiest for her to go to school. Older children and adolescents often tell me that they would go to school as long as they didn't have to attend one or two key classes such as gym or English class. So I tell them: go to school except for gym and English class! Find out what time of day your child is willing to go to school and use that as a starting point. Then you and she can gradually increase the amount of time spent in school.

If your child is missing most or all of the school day, then first pursuing a part-time schedule is a good idea. As mentioned in chapter 3, the first step in a part-time schedule can involve one of the following:

- Your child goes to school in the morning and is then allowed to come home within an hour (then gradually work forward by adding more time).

- Your child goes to school at 2 p.m. and is then allowed to come home when school normally ends, say at 3:10 p.m. (then gradually work backward by adding more time).

- Your child goes to school only for lunch and is then allowed to come home afterward (then gradually add more school time before and after lunch).

- Your child goes to school only for her favorite class or time of day (then gradually add more classes or school time).

- Your child attends a school room other than his classroom, such as the school library, guidance counselor or nurse's office, or main lobby (then gradually add more classroom time).

Because I covered these steps at length in chapter 3, I will not repeat myself here. However, if your child is missing most of the school day, then I invite you to read chapter 3 and, in particular, the section on changing the "doing" part of distress. This section will give you more detailed ideas about how to set up a part-time attendance schedule that will eventually lead to full-time attendance. Be sure your child practices changing the "feeling" and "thinking" parts of distress even during the part-time school schedule. If your child does go to school for most of the day but has trouble skipping one or two classes or being in different social or performance situations at school, then read the next section.

Trouble in Social and Performance Situations at School

If your child is skipping a key class or two, such as gym class, or goes to school but has a lot of distress about social or performance situations when there, then this section is for you. If your child is skipping one or two classes, be sure that she continues to go to school for the other classes. In addition, arrange with school officials some place that your child can go, other than hiding out in the bathroom or some other place, during the skipped classes. If your child will not go to gym class, for example, arrange so that she can spend the time (for now) in the school library or guidance counselor's office. That way she is at least supervised and you can monitor how much time she spent in class. Gradually more time in gym class can be scheduled later.

Many kids are nervous about tests and have trouble going to classes when tests are scheduled. In this case, try to get sample tests from different teachers that your child can practice at school or home. As your child is

Gym Class

One of the toughest classes for many older children and adolescents to attend is gym or physical education class. Many kids do not like physical education because they have to change clothes or shower before others, perform athletically before others, and risk being teased, ridiculed, embarrassed, or picked last for a team. As a result, some kids skip gym class or do not participate very much during the class.

If this applies to your child, work with her on the methods described in this chapter. Be sure that your child is relaxed and help change negative thoughts she may have during gym class. If your child is not participating much in gym class, try to work on ways that she can talk to others and get more involved with the sports that are being conducted. If your child is teased or ridiculed or always picked last for a team, talk to the physical education teacher to see how this might be resolved. Perhaps your child can occasionally be chosen to pick a team, or a lottery system could be set up where teams are chosen randomly. If your child is embarrassed about how she performs at a sport, practice the sport with her.

A particularly tough problem involves not wanting to undress or shower in the locker room. Do not allow your child to avoid this or to get dressed in a private location. Instead, ask your child to be as prepared as possible with his gear. This means bringing all necessary clothes and getting changed for class as efficiently as possible. In addition, encourage your child to speak to others in the locker room and during gym class so his focus is on making eye contact and starting and joining conversations, and not on worry about being watched or judged.

practicing these tests, time the tests just as they would be timed in school. In addition, have your child practice methods for relaxing and for changing negative thoughts described in this chapter. Talk to your child about what thoughts she may be having during the first 5 minutes of the sample test. Many youths worry, for example, about failing or "freezing up." If this is the case, be sure to help your child physically relax and think realistically using questions such as, "Are you 100% sure you will fail or freeze?," "What is the worst thing that could happen if you did fail or freeze?," and "Are you the only person who is nervous about taking this test?"

As your child practices sample tests and becomes better at them, then arrange with your child's guidance counselor and teachers to begin practice tests in the classroom. These can involve tests that are done after school or during some time of day when other people are not around. The tests may or may not count toward your child's actual grade, but the important thing is that your child is practicing the tests and taking them with less distress. Later on, as your child becomes better at taking these tests, then she can start taking them during her regularly scheduled classes. *Be sure that you continue to rate your child's distress using the worksheet provided in chapter 2 so you can see whether progress is being made.*

The same can be done for other situations that older children and adolescents sometimes avoid. For example:

- Have your child practice oral presentations or write on a blackboard at home or in an empty classroom before doing so in a full classroom setting.

- Have your child practice playing a musical instrument before a small group of people, such as relatives, friends, or immediate family members, before doing so in front of larger audiences.

- Have your child practice asking and answering questions with a teacher when no one is around before doing so in class.

- Have your child practice other performances that make her nervous, such as driving, eating in a cafeteria, using public restrooms, undressing and showering with people nearby, and walking into school or class.

As your child practices these situations, be sure to help her relax and change negative thoughts to more realistic ones. Continue to rate your child's level of distress in these situations. Many kids need a lot of practice in these situations before they feel completely comfortable, so be patient and persistent. In addition, reward your child for practicing these different tasks.

What about social situations at school? As mentioned earlier, many children are shy and have trouble speaking to other kids at school. If this is so for your child, then she needs to practice different kinds of social situations, such as the following:

- Walking up to others to ask a question

- Starting a conversation in a relaxed area such as the cafeteria, bus, playground, or extracurricular activity

Extracurricular Activities

Extracurricular activities are school-related clubs, groups, teams, and other peer gatherings where kids share a common interest and can make new friends. Extracurricular activities can actually have a strong impact on school attendance. Many youths have trouble going to school because they feel isolated, lonely, and "on the outside looking in." They may be in a racial minority, new to a school, or shy in general. As a result, they sometimes do not feel motivated to go to class. If this applies to your child, then one way to change this is to get her more involved in extracurricular activities so she can develop friends who might share her classes.

As a first step, get a list of available extracurricular activities from your child's guidance counselor or knowledgeable school official. Then sit down and talk to your child about which activities interest her the most. Do not let your child get away with saying "none of these." Some activities will be more liked than others, and your child can try those first. I recommend that your child try at least three activities for a month. That way, even if one or two don't work out, another is still available. Also, encourage your child to make friends with peers in these groups. Encourage her to call these other kids on the telephone, make plans to see a movie, or invite them over for dinner.

On the other hand, be careful not to overload your child with too many extracurricular activities. Some children refuse school because they are so overwhelmed with schoolwork, a part-time job, a sports team, and several other activities such as piano or karate lessons. If this is the case, then ask your child where some time might be saved, and then allow her to gradually withdraw from some commitments.

- Asking someone to stop doing something annoying

- Joining a group of kids who are already playing together

- Calling a classmate on the telephone to get a homework assignment

- Asking and answering questions in class

Like performance situations, these social situations can be practiced outside of school in comfortable places like home or in a church group. You can even act out different situations for your child, such as pretending to be the teacher as your child has to ask a question. As your child does this, let her know what could be done a little differently to be more effective. For example, your child may have to speak more clearly, make better eye contact, and pause a little before responding.

A reminder: If your child has a great deal of trouble with these situations, then seeking the help of a qualified mental health professional may be necessary (see chapter 1). The recommendations made in this chapter are for older children and adolescents who have some *but not severe* trouble attending school due to distress about social or performance situations there. In addition, the methods described here must be done with the cooperation of school officials. Solving the problem of school refusal behavior takes the effort of everyone working together—you, your child, and your child's school.

Do's and Don'ts!

I know that I have given you a lot of information in this chapter. Here is a list of some do and don't reminders.

Do:

- Help your child understand the different parts of distress: the physical "feelings," "thinking," and "doing" parts of distress.

- Think about how these different parts of distress occur in your child.

- Teach your child correct breathing by using deep, slow, diaphragmatic breathing.

- Teach your child to relax her muscles using the tense-and-release method.

- Encourage your child to relax in general and give her feedback about doing so.

- Work nightly with your child to help her think more realistically in social and performance situations.

- Work with your child to practice social and performance situations that he or she has difficulty with.

- Work closely with school officials.

- Set up a part-time school attendance schedule if necessary.

- Seek support from others.

- Be consistent and use these methods every day.

Don't:

- Fight, yell, lecture, criticize, negotiate, beg, or bribe your child to go to school.

- Ignore your child's distress.

- Use statements such as, "Don't worry," "Snap out of it," "There's nothing to be afraid of," "You're not really upset," or "You're faking it."

- Allow your child to come home early or do fun things during school hours.

Final Comments

Having a child who is distressed about school and who is missing school can be very upsetting, but the problem is fixable! Lowering a child's distress about social and performance situations demands a lot of practice. Keep practicing those situations that give your child difficulty until she can do them well. Also, be patient, seek support from others in your life, and cooperate with school officials who can help. You can do it!

Children Who Refuse School

for Attention

■ *Sam is an 8-year-old boy who has problems attending school because he would much rather be with his mother at home. Sam often refuses to go to school in the morning, although his mom (Emily) can sometimes get him to go into the school building. Sam says he likes school but often misses his mother. Whenever he is at school, Sam tries to call Emily and has even run out of the school building twice to try to go home. Lately, Emily has been eating lunch with Sam in the school cafeteria to get him to go to school with less fuss.* ■

This chapter will be *more helpful* to you if your child matches Sam's situation or if one or more of the following is true:

- Your child is refusing school *only* to get attention from you or significant others.

- Your child wants you to attend school with him.

- Your family's morning routine is chaotic.

- Your child is having trouble attending school mostly in the mornings.

- Your child is exaggerating physical complaints (stomachaches, headaches) to try to stay out of school.

- Your child has trouble separating from you or significant others.

This chapter will be *less helpful* to you if one or more of the following is true:

- Your child is refusing school *only* because he is very distressed about something related to school (see chapter 3).

- Your child is refusing school *only* because he is very distressed about social or performance situations at school (see chapter 4).

- Your child is refusing school *only* to do more fun activities outside of school (see chapter 6).

Children Who Refuse School for Attention

In chapter 2 we discussed different reasons why children have trouble going to school. One reason is that some children, like Sam, seek a lot of attention from one or both parents and are defiant about going to school because they would rather stay home. In Sam's case, for example, he often resisted going to school in the morning because he wanted to spend the day helping his mom (Emily) around the house or going with her to her part-time job. He was not upset about school but insisted that Emily be at school during part of the day.

Children who refuse school for attention are often younger and may have temper tantrums in the morning, say they want to stay home from school or have a parent go to school with them, and show stubborn, willful, manipulative, or guilt-inducing behavior to try to stay home. If these children do go to school, they may constantly call their parents during the day, persistently ask the same questions over and over, and even run away from the school building to try to get home. Many of these children are *not particularly distressed* about school. If you feel that your child *is* distressed about school, however, then be sure to read chapters 3 and 4.

To change your child's attention-seeking behavior and help improve his school attendance, I will concentrate on the following:

- Setting up a regular morning routine

- Paying attention to appropriate behaviors and ignoring inappropriate behaviors

- Setting up formal rewards for going to school without a fuss

- Setting up formal punishments for going to school with a fuss

- Changing what you say to your child

- Dealing with excessive telephone calls and questions

- Dealing with a child who runs away from the school building

- Forcing a child to attend school under certain circumstances

Why Am I Doing This?

If your child resembles Sam, my guess is that he is pretty much in control of your family's morning routine. He may be "calling the shots," and everyone else in the family is kind of reacting to what he does in the morning. For example, you may be waiting for your child to throw a temper tantrum and trying to do whatever you can to prevent it, like allowing him to watch television when he really should be getting a backpack together for school.

In addition, you may be "working with" your child to try to get him to go to school. You may be yelling, lecturing, negotiating, bribing, or constantly bugging your child to go to school. You may be trying to comfort his minor physical complaints or you may keep responding to his constant statements and questions about wanting to stay home. In the meantime, he is still resisting going to school or missing school! You are basically *reacting* to what your child is doing and, in doing so, giving him a lot of attention that reinforces his school refusal behaviors (figure 5.1). I call this "dancing to the child's tune." What ways do you think you might be reacting to your child's behavior or doing extra work to help him out in the morning?

We have to change this. Your child should be dancing to *your* tune (figure 5.2). In other words, we have to set up the morning so that your child is responding to *your* rules and to what *you* say, and not the other way around. To do this, we have to set up a clear and predictable morning routine that your child is expected to follow *each school day*. If he follows this routine, then good things (rewards) will happen. If he does not follow this routine, then less-than-good things (punishments) will happen. In this way, your child will be responding to rules and consequences that *you* are putting in place. You are the boss!

Figure 5.1
Responding to your child's school refusal behavior ("dancing to his tune")

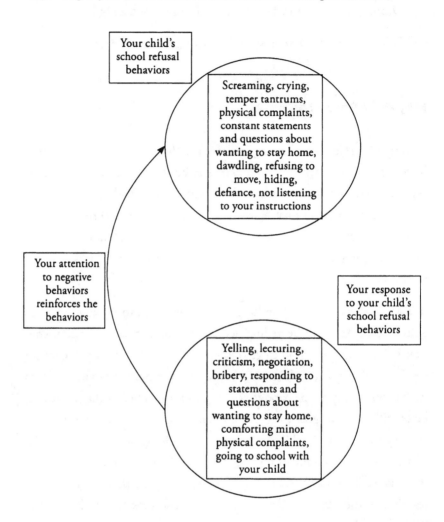

Getting your child to dance to your tune also means giving your child commands that are short and to the point. I am sure you are tired of lengthy arguments, reassurances, and promises to get your child to go to school. I will help you make *simple commands* to your child that he clearly understands and must comply with. Again, if he does comply with these commands, then good things (rewards) will happen. If he does not comply with these commands, then less-than-good things (punishments) will happen. In this way, your child will be responding to *your* statements.

Getting your child to dance to your tune also means setting *boundaries* on his behavior. So, I will also discuss what child behaviors to ignore and which to attend to in the morning, what physical symptoms should allow

Figure 5.2
Responding to your rules and statements ("dancing to your tune")

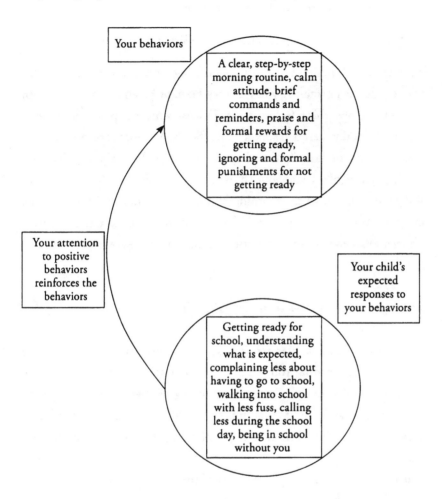

Your behaviors

A clear, step-by-step morning routine, calm attitude, brief commands and reminders, praise and formal rewards for getting ready, ignoring and formal punishments for not getting ready

Your attention to positive behaviors reinforces the behaviors

Your child's expected responses to your behaviors

Getting ready for school, understanding what is expected, complaining less about having to go to school, walking into school with less fuss, calling less during the school day, being in school without you

a child to stay home from school, what to say to a child who asks the same questions over and over, how to handle frequent telephone calls from your child during the day, when to (and not to) go to school with your child, and what to do if your child runs away from the school building. I will also cover the topic of forcing your child to go to school.

All of these recommendations will require a lot of effort on your part. The methods in this chapter will be helpful *only* if you and/or your spouse/partner:

- Have the *will and the ability* to carry out the methods

- Support each other

- Are confident that your child is refusing school *only* for attention

- Are working closely with school officials

- Can commit to doing the methods consistently and permanently

If you feel a little hesitant or guilty about doing some of the methods in this chapter, that is normal. If you feel very hesitant or guilty, however, then you must resolve these feelings first. Discuss whatever plan you develop with adult family members and school officials. Most importantly, keep in mind that the methods in this chapter are designed to help improve your family's quality of life and your child's quality of life. Your family's quality of life will improve as the morning becomes easier and as the air become less tense. Your child's quality of life will improve as he more easily attends school and receives a good education. In the long run, everybody wins!

Setting Up a Regular Morning Routine

If you have a child who is refusing school for attention, or if you have a very chaotic morning routine before school starts, then *the first thing* we have to do is set up a *structured morning routine*. Many parents say that weekday mornings are their most stressful and difficult times of their week, especially when their child is complaining of physical symptoms and constantly asking to stay home. Many parents say their morning routine is rushed, disorganized, and hectic. Part of the reason for this, of course, is that a child is dawdling, refusing to move, or throwing a temper tantrum to try to stay home from school.

We have to change this. *Your first step* is to sit down this evening to plan the morning routine in peace and quiet. All adults in the house must be in

> *Prepare a morning routine that will be the same each morning.*

on this plan! *Your second step* is to prepare a morning routine that will be the same each morning. Although different things come up each day, try to keep the same schedule each weekday morning. When a child knows what is expected of him each day and what consequences (rewards and punishments) will follow, then there is less need for constant explaining from parents and fighting among family members.

I recommend that your child rise from bed about 120 minutes before the beginning of school. If your child is expected to enter the school building at 8:50 a.m., for example, then he should be out of bed by 6:50 a.m. This is the example I am using here, but you will have to use whatever times apply most to you. In addition, I am assuming you have a short drive of no more than 10 minutes to your child's school (or your child's bus ride is no more than 10 minutes long). If the commute is longer, then please budget for this extra time by having your child get up even earlier.

If your child is expected to rise at, say 6:50 a.m., then his alarm (which may be you) should go off at 6:30, 6:40, and 6:48 a.m. Your child should awake at 6:30, again at 6:40, and again at 6:48 and then be expected to arise from bed at 6:50 a.m. If he does not rise from bed, then you will need to help him do so. You can also remind your child that some consequence (reward or punishment) will follow if he gets out of bed or fails to get out of bed on time (see later section).

The next step in planning the morning routine is to list the preparations that your child is expected to do to get ready for school. These preparations should be listed in the order that *you want*, and each should be given a certain number of minutes to complete. For example:

6:50 a.m.	Rise from bed
6:50–7 a.m.	Go to the bathroom and wash (10 minutes)
7–7:20 a.m.	Eat breakfast (which should be ready by 7 or whenever breakfast time starts) (20 minutes)
7:20–7:30 a.m.	Brush teeth in bathroom and wash as needed (10 minutes)
7:30–7:50 a.m.	Dress and accessorize for school (20 minutes)
7:45–8 a.m.	Make final preparation for school such as putting on a jacket or getting backpack ready) (15 minutes)
8–8:20 a.m.	Extra time (if child is ready, provide some reward at this time; if child is not ready, he can use this time to finish) (20 minutes)

8:20–8:40 a.m.   Commute to school (20 minutes)

8:40–8:50 a.m.   Final goodbyes and child enters school (10 minutes)

Be sure to give your child more time than is needed to complete each step. I recommend that you give your child plenty of time to complete each step, *and then add 5 minutes.* For example, if you feel your son can easily dress for school in 10 minutes but often needs 15 minutes because of dawdling, then give him 20 minutes to finish dressing. If your morning routine is flexible like this, then problems such as temper tantrums or dawdling will have less effect. For example, if your child took 13 minutes instead of 10 minutes to go to the bathroom and wash, then this places a little bit of pressure but not a lot of pressure on the next step because extra time for the next step is already built in. In this way, your morning routine is not as rushed because plenty of time is provided for each step.

Build into your morning routine a "buffer zone" of extra time. In the routine listed above, for example, "extra time" takes place from 8 to 8:20 a.m. If your son completed all of the morning routine steps and is ready by this time, then some reward (see later section) should be given. For example, he could be allowed to watch a cartoon on television or read a book. If your child has *not* completed all of the morning routine steps by this time, then the extra time can be used to make sure everything is ready. For example, if your son dawdled and finally got everything ready by 8:15 a.m., then you are still on schedule for bringing him to school. However, this dawdling will have to be punished later that evening (see later section).

The routine I have provided here is only an example. You must develop your own routine that is best for you. For example, you may have other children to consider. Or you may prefer a different routine or other step such as your child taking a shower. Or one adult in the house might have to leave for work in the middle of your child's morning routine, so extra time for each step after that person leaves needs to be budgeted. If your spouse/partner leaves for work *before or during* your child's morning routine, then be sure to budget a lot of extra time for each step. To develop your morning routine, use the worksheet that is provided (worksheet 5.1). Because your morning routine may change slightly from week to week, feel free to photocopy this worksheet or download multiple copies from the companion Web site at www.oup.com/us/schoolrefusal.

Worksheet 5.1

Our Morning Routine

What I want my child to do

Time to complete
this step (e.g., 7–7:20 a.m.)

_____   _____

_____   _____

_____   _____

_____   _____

_____   _____

_____   _____

_____   _____

After you create the morning routine, be sure to share it with everyone in the house, including all children and especially the child who is having trouble attending school. You may ask for input, but do not negotiate the morning routine with your child. *You are setting up a house rule that must be obeyed.*

> *Do not negotiate the morning routine with your child.*

After the morning routine has been finalized, try it out for a couple of days. Do this to see what needs tweaking. For example, you may find that one particular step needs more time, so the morning routine can be changed slightly to accommodate this. After a couple of days of tweaking, however, your morning routine should be set.

A clear and regular morning routine is the foundation for the methods discussed in this chapter. Everything else we discuss flows from this routine. All of the other things I will ask you to practice will be made much easier if the morning routine is set and everyone knows what is expected. Again, this routine must be practiced consistently each school morning! No exceptions unless some emergency arises! *If you feel you cannot manage the morning routine by yourself, then you must find someone to help you.* For example, someone could help get the other kids to school as you focus on your child with school refusal behavior.

Paying Attention to Appropriate Behaviors and Ignoring Inappropriate Behaviors

If your child is like Sam, then he probably receives a lot of attention for refusing to go to school. This is understandable. We as parents sometimes find ourselves lecturing, yelling, cajoling, and begging our children to go to school. When this happens occasionally, it is not too bad. When this happens almost every day, however, it becomes a problem that we must solve.

You may find that you are currently giving your child a lot of attention, even negative attention, for behaviors such as dawdling, refusing to move, physical complaints, or crying. You may feel frustrated when your child will not go to school and naturally turn that frustration into anger toward your child. This has not worked, however. Instead, we have to try a different way.

During the morning routine and as you bring your child to school, *pay attention to appropriate behaviors* such as completing each step of the morning routine and getting on the bus or into the car without a fuss. If your child responds well to the morning routine and the other suggestions in this chapter, then be sure to let him know you are happy. Remember that we are talking about a child who likes attention from you. Catch your child being good and praise him for doing what you like.

When your child does something in the morning that you like, such as getting dressed on time, be sure to smile, verbally praise, or hug your child as he is completing the morning tasks. Tell your child, for example, "I like the way you are dressing yourself" or "Great job eating your breakfast!" Do not take any positive behavior for granted — *reward your child often when he is doing even minor things that help the process of going to school.* Of course, you cannot reward every little thing your child does during the morning, but sprinkle your attention throughout the morning so your child feels rewarded and motivated to get ready for school.

> *Catch your child being good and praise him for doing what you like.*

As much as possible, also try to ignore *inappropriate behaviors* such as dawdling, crying, minor physical complaints, and temper tantrums. I know this is often hard to do. The idea, however, is to let your child know that he has to prepare for school despite any problems he has in doing so. You should draw your attention away from behaviors that we do not want to see. In that way, the behaviors will not be rewarded and they should lessen. Ignoring inappropriate behaviors will take some work on your part because it may not be what you are used to doing. You must practice this!

Have other people help you with this by reminding you when you should be ignoring a certain behavior.

What about physical complaints? We certainly do not want to ignore real symptoms, but I recommend that a child go to school *except* when there is:

- A temperature of 100 degrees or more

- Frequent vomiting

- Bleeding

- Lice

- Severe diarrhea

- Severe flu-like symptoms

- Another very severe medical condition such as intense pain

If your child has these problems, seek the advice of your pediatrician (see chapter 3 for more information on physical complaints). Even under these circumstances, however, some children can go to school. For example, your child may vomit or have diarrhea in the morning before school but not at school. In this case, he can still be expected to go to school. A good idea is to assume that your child is going to school and that only extreme circumstances, such as high temperature, will allow you to even consider letting a child stay home from school. Try to build this expectation in *your child*: yes, you are going to school today!

Setting Up Formal Rewards for Going to School Without a Fuss

Paying attention to good morning behaviors is very important, but there is even more you can do to encourage your child to prepare for and go to school—*formal rewards*. Formal rewards include things a child can touch and see, such as watching television or playing a game. Formal rewards can be given in the morning *and* the evening. If your child has completed the morning routine without any problems, then use the morning "buffer time" to give formal rewards. For example, a child who is ready by 8 a.m. and who does not have to leave the house until 8:30 a.m. can be allowed to play, read, watch television, or do some fun (though brief) activity with you. You should be ready by this time as well (say, 8) so that you have time to give your child formal rewards as they are needed.

If your child prepares for school, leaves the house, and goes to school without any behavior problems such as temper tantrums, then be sure to provide some reward during the evening. Again, because these children like attention, good rewards include staying up a little later, doing fun activities with a parent, reading stories together, running errands together, or walking the dog together. Be sure during this time to remind your child why he is getting this reward—that going to school without a fuss means good things! *Also, be sure to give some reward, even a little one, every day your child goes to school without a fuss.*

Setting Up Formal Punishments for Going to School With a Fuss

Okay, we have talked about the carrots, so now we have to talk about the sticks. What happens if your child *does have trouble* getting through the morning routine and going to school? If this is the case, the first thing you should check is whether the morning routine you have set up is too difficult for your child. If you feel this might be so, then tweak the routine so that your child has plenty of time to complete each step.

The second thing you should do is decide which of your child's morning behaviors are most challenging for you—that is, what *specifically* does your child do in the morning to drive you nuts? Many parents answer this question by giving general statements such as "not going to school" or "goofing around." But what I want you to do is think about *very specific behavior problems* that your child shows in the morning. Some of these behaviors may come from the worksheet I gave you regarding morning problems (see chapter 2 and worksheet 2.4). Continue to keep a checklist of these behaviors each day and pick which ones seem most challenging.

I recommend that you start by picking *two behavior problems* that are most challenging for you. Focus on punishing these two behavior problems first. Once they lessen, then other behavior problems can be punished as well. These behavior problems will likely include:

- Not finishing or not even trying the morning routine (including a lot of dawdling)

- Temper tantrums that involve crying, screaming, kicking, or flailing of arms and legs

- Refusing to move, such as not leaving bed, the house, or the car

- Refusing to enter the school building

- Running away from home or the school building

All of these morning behavior problems, and others that you may have listed, interfere with your child's ability to go to school on time. Therefore, the behaviors *must be punished*. The purpose of punishment is not to hurt a child or vent a parent's anger but rather to *clearly teach a child* what behaviors are expected and rewarded and which behaviors are unacceptable and punishable. When done correctly and with rewards for good behavior, punishment can be an effective tool for shaping a child's behavior. Remember, we are setting up a system where your child dances to *your* tune!

Many parents say they do not like punishing their child for problems going to school. This is understandable. Punishment can sometimes be a hard and unpleasant thing to do. However, we are talking about a child who *should be going to school* and *who is not distressed* about school. If your son refused to pick up his jacket after you told him to do so, I am sure you would find this unacceptable. School refusal behavior for attention is the same thing. Your child should be listening to what you say about going to school but is not. We have to change this.

As with rewards, punishments can occur in the morning and evening. Punishing a child in the morning as he is refusing to get ready can be a little tricky. Sometimes punishment for an attention-seeking child can be as simple as ignoring a temper tantrum or screaming fit (see earlier section). I recommend that you try to ignore these kinds of acting-out (disruptive) behaviors in the morning as much as possible. Instead, continue with your routine and act as if going to school and work is expected.

If your child knows that acting-out (disruptive) behaviors such as tantrums will not get any attention, he is less likely to continue the behaviors. If you are ignoring this kind of behavior, then you might wish to put an egg timer nearby to let your child know how many minutes he has left to complete a certain step in the morning routine, such as getting dressed. That way you are giving your child feedback about what he needs to do, but you are not giving extra verbal attention to the tantrum or screaming.

Punishment in the morning can also involve loss of "free time." If your son is not ready by 8, for example, then he will have to use his extra "buffer time" you built into your morning routine to finish getting ready. If he has been throwing a temper tantrum, you can also restrict the kinds of activities he does during this free time. For example, you could tell him that he loses television time during the free time because he was screaming and saying, "No!" However, if he is ready by 8 despite the screaming fit, he may lose television but still be permitted some other activity such as reading.

Punishments for poor behavior should also occur in the evening. *My rule of thumb is that punishment should last double the number of minutes that a child was disruptive in the morning.* For example, if a child's temper tantrum lasted 10 minutes in the morning, then the evening punishment should last 20 minutes. In addition, if a child completed the morning routine but then refused to enter the school building for 15 minutes, then the evening punishment should last 30 minutes. If a child was late finishing the morning routine by 7 minutes, then the evening punishment should last 14 minutes. These punishments would be in addition to any given in the morning.

I recommend punishments that involve some loss of attention from you. Examples include having to go to bed early, losing an activity with a parent, and having to stay in one's room or sit on the stairs. I do not recommend physical punishment because loss of attention is usually more effective with these younger children. Besides, you may have already discovered that physical punishment has not really helped your child's school attendance, and many parents do not want to give physical punishment every single day. If you use physical punishment, I recommend you use it only for dangerous behaviors such as running out of the house and into the street.

If your child misses many of the steps in the morning routine or has many problems entering school, then much of the evening will serve as punishment time. "Yikes," you might say! But this sounds worse than it is. What I mean is that a child who was very disruptive in the morning before school should spend the evening without privileges such as television, videogames, telephone calls, computer time, or playing with friends. Instead, have your child complete chores around the house, do schoolwork, and go to bed early. In addition, tell your child that tomorrow is a new day and that better things will happen if he goes to school without a fuss.

Some parents tell me that their child has built up a huge amount of minutes that are owed in punishment. For example, a child may have completely refused to go to school for a week and now owes his parents many hours of punishment time. If this is the case, allow your child to do something on the weekend as "community service" to clean the slate. For example, ask your child to clean the garage, weed the yard, or wash the windows (all with your help and supervision) for a full morning. Once your child has done this, tell him the slate is now clean and that you expect him to go to school on Monday.

Do not threaten extreme punishments! Some parents believe that one large punishment will motivate a child to go to school, and this may actually work once or twice but not forever. Some parents, for example, threaten to cancel a child's birthday party, take away all social activities for a month, or not celebrate a holiday such as Halloween or Christmas. There are some big problems with this. First, you cannot do extreme punishments every day, and many kids do refuse school daily. Second, most parents back off their threats to do something this drastic, which hurts their credibility: why would a child listen to such threats if they are never carried out? Besides, could you or would you really want to carry out these kinds of punishments?

The best punishments for school refusal behavior are those that are basic and those that are done daily and consistently. Remember that your child likes attention from you, so the best punishments will involve your disappointment and lack of attention. Do not shun your child, but do make it clear that you expect him to make better choices and to go to school. *And do not forget to praise and give rewards for positive behaviors such as completing the morning routine!* Carrots *and* sticks, not either alone, will work best for school refusal behavior.

Changing What You Say to Your Child

At this point I know you have a lot to do: you must create and manage the morning routine and give rewards and punishments when needed. On top of all this, however, I must ask you to do something else. This has to do with what you say to your child in the morning and how you say it. In general, I am going to ask you to speak in short, clear sentences with a tone of voice that is calm and matter-of-fact.

When your child is refusing to go to school, or refusing to do anything else, there is always the temptation to lecture your way out of the situation! Believe me, I know. Many parents go on and on with their child about how his behavior is hurting them or about how bad he is being. Other parents criticize their children or yell at them for not going to school. Still other parents make the mistake of bargaining with their children, promising them wonderful things if they just go to school! Unfortunately, these practices do not work.

We have to do something else. When you speak to your child in the morning, or tell him something to do (a command), please keep the following in mind:

- Tell your child exactly what you want him to do.

- Give short, direct commands.

- Make direct eye contact when speaking to your child or giving him a command.

- Make sure your child can actually do what you are asking.

- Do a task with your child.

- Reward good listening and punish poor listening.

Let's talk about these in more detail. When you want your child to do something, *be very, very specific!* Parents often tell their children to "clean their room" or "get ready for school," but these statements are unclear. Your idea of a clean room and your child's idea of a clean room may be very different! So, try more specific statements such as "pick up your clothes from the floor within 5 minutes" and "put your books in your backpack right now." An advantage of saying something like this is that your child understands what you want and it will be easy for you to check to see that it was done. Being specific in your commands will also make it easy for you to know if a reward or punishment is needed. If your son did not put his books into his backpack, for example, then it's pretty clear he didn't listen to you and deserves some punishment.

When giving a command to your child, be *very brief* in what you say. No lecturing! No criticizing! No sarcasm! And no questions! Do not, for example, say something like, "Will you please just eat your breakfast?" Instead, say "You've got 5 minutes to eat your breakfast" or "Put your pants on now." Keep your commands brief and do not keep repeating yourself. If your child listened to your command, give praise. If your child did not listen to your command, then the punishments you have already set up will automatically kick in.

When you give a command to your child, make sure you have his undivided attention. Do not give a command when your child is preoccupied with watching television, reading a magazine, or talking to someone else. Instead, say to your child, "Look at me," get his full attention, and then give your command. Also, if you are unsure whether your child fully listened or understood what you just said, then ask him to repeat what you just said. You can see why I want you to budget plenty of time for the morning routine!

Make sure as well that you are giving your child commands that he can actually do. One mistake parents make is to load their child with things to do and then get frustrated when everything is not done. A parent might say, for example, "Go into your room, get dressed, brush your teeth, and comb your hair." Ten minutes later, when the boy is dressed but just sitting on his bed, his father might become upset! A better way to do this is to give your child *one step to do at a time.* For example, you could say, "Go into your room and get dressed now" and then check on your child 10 minutes later to give the next command ("Good job. Now go brush your teeth."). And so on. Remember that a 7- or 8-year-old does not think and remember the way you do, so keep it simple!

I also suggest that you do with your child whatever you want him to do. For example, brush your teeth together, get dressed at the same time, eat breakfast together, and pack up briefcases/purses and backpacks together. If you keep the same general routine as your child, you can better monitor how well he is doing. Also, you will serve as a good model for when that step should be done. And most kids, especially those who like attention, certainly enjoy doing things (even little things) with their parents.

During the morning routine and as your child goes to school, be sure to praise and give formal rewards for good behavior and punishments for poor behavior. In addition, be sure to maintain your voice in an even and calm manner. Try not to get upset or raise your voice. Instead, adopt a neutral, low-key, matter-of-fact tone. I like to think of it as the "You're going to school, end of story" tone. No fighting, no arguing, no begging—just the simple expectation that your child is going to school no matter what. End of story. Doing so will get across to your child your expectation that he should complete the morning routine and go to school. Do not yell or threaten your child; let the rewards and punishments that you set up beforehand do your talking for you. Your child is dancing to *your* tune!

Dealing With Repeated Statements/Questions and Telephone Calls

You may find, even after the morning routine is in place and your child is going to school, that he is still constantly pestering you with the same questions over and over or calling you constantly from school. Children who refuse school for attention often do these kinds of things. For example, they may continually whine in the morning and say things like, "I don't want to go to school. Can't I just stay home today? Mom, I want to stay home today. Please! I want to stay with you" and on and on and on. How draining.

Constantly responding to these repeated statements and questions will wear you out, so don't do it. Respond *once* to your child's statement or question about school. You can say something like, "Yes, we've talked about this before. You are going to school today. End of story." *After that, ignore your child's repeated statements and questions.* When you continue to respond, the attention you are giving only reinforces your child's behavior. Ignoring the behavior will help reduce these statements and questions over time.

What about persistent telephone calls to you from school? Many kids now bring cell phones to school and make many calls home or to a parent's workplace. If this is the case for you, then set a clear limit about how many times your child can call you and under what circumstances. I recommend that your child call you no more than twice per day (once in the morning and once in the afternoon) and *only* during times when the call is allowed at school and does not interfere with classroom activity. Check with school officials to see when a good time for a call would be.

In addition, your child should be allowed to call you *only* if he is having a good day at school, so I recommend setting up these calls *only after* you have talked to your child's teacher or guidance counselor. Also, if your child is calling to try to get out of school or to ask you to pick him up early, then do not allow this. Simply tell your child that he must stay in school and that you will pick him up (or see him later) at the usual time. If necessary, end the call yourself. If your child keeps calling inappropriately, then be sure to punish this behavior later that evening.

Dealing With a Child Who Runs Away From the School Building

I confess that the behavior that worries me the most is a child's willingness to run out of the school building. Most children who refuse school for attention do spend the entire day in the classroom *once they are there*. Other kids, though, look to run out the door or slip away from the playground and go down the street. Some of these kids hide, but many try to find their way home. Of course, this is an extremely dangerous behavior that must be addressed as soon as it happens!

If you feel your child may run away from the school building, then you must meet with school officials immediately. This meeting should include a member of your school's police force if one is available. *Keep in mind three main things*. First, be sure a plan is put in place that involves greater monitoring of your child during the school day. Once school officials know that a child is a "flight risk," they should take extra precautions to make sure this child does not leave the school building early again. Make sure you are comfortable with whatever plan is proposed, but I recommend the plan *at least* include adult escorts from class to other areas of the school building, someone waiting for your child outside the restroom, and teachers or others keeping an "eagle eye" on your child during lunch, recess, and other non-classroom times.

Second, develop a plan for what happens if your child does somehow leave the school campus. I recommend that school police or regular police officers be notified as soon as possible if this occurs. You should obviously be notified immediately as well. If your child does somehow make it home and you are there, bring him back to school and let school officials know where he is and what happened. Then investigate what went wrong and how it could be prevented in the future.

Third, let school officials know when your child is going to be absent on a given day. That way, they won't be looking for your child if he is not there. In addition, make it a habit of going to the front office to let someone in charge know that your child is now in school, even if he is late. The goal is to set up a system where you and school officials always know where your child is and, if he is not where he is supposed to be, then making sure that everyone knows right away what has happened so he can be found.

■ *Separation Anxiety and "Clingy" Behavior*

Most of this chapter has been devoted to your child's attention-seeking behavior, which is a main problem seen in children who refuse school. As I mentioned in chapter 2, however, some of these kids also have separation anxiety, which refers to a lot of worry about harm happening to parents or to the child when separation occurs. Many kids with separation anxiety, for example, worry about their parents being in a car accident and not being able to pick them up from school.

If your child has separation anxiety, he may insist that you be at school by a certain time to pick him up. Many kids insist, for example, that their parent pick them up at a very specific time, such as 3:17 p.m. Many parents will respond to this by making sure they are there by 3:17 p.m. and even moving around their afternoon schedule to accommodate this. If you are doing something like this, however, you are "dancing to your child's tune" instead of the other way around.

Children have to learn to be flexible and learn that terrible things are not likely to happen if a parent is a few minutes late picking them up. If your child has this issue, then ask him to wait for you at a safe spot at school.

Examples include the main office or lobby, school playground, or front door. Tell your child that you will not be more than 15 minutes late but that you will pick him up at different times. So, if your child is ready by 3:17 p.m., you will be there anytime between 3:17 p.m. and 3:32 p.m. Then, vary the times that you pick your child up. Come one day at 3:22, another day at 3:30, and another day at 3:17 p.m. (it's okay to be on time occasionally!). Ignore tantrums and complaints about this.

When you do pick up your child from school, remind him that nothing bad happened. As you practice this more, your child will become less tense and realize that bad things are not likely to happen. As he can tolerate these different times, be sure to praise him for being brave. Also, in case you are ever later than 3:32 p.m., give your child a strategy for what to do. I recommend that your child speak to someone in the main office about the fact you are late (only past 3:32 p.m. in this example). That way, he will feel safe until you or someone else does come to pick him up. If your child has a cell phone, then you can call and tell him that you will be there a little past 3:32 p.m. (or whatever time applies to your situation).

Other kids with separation anxiety cling tightly to their parents in the morning. Some of this behavior is for attention and some of it is due to distress. However, your response should be the same. If your child clings to you on the playground before school, set up a regular routine for the drop-off just as you did for the morning at home. For example:

- Arrive at the school playground at the same time each school day, and preferably 10 minutes before your child is expected to enter the school building.

- Ask your child in the car if he has everything ready for school. Ask this question as well before you leave the house, so the answer in the car should always be "yes." Do not allow your child an excuse to go back home; if something was forgotten, tell your child that he has to go to school on time but that you will bring the item to school later. If you do this, bring the item to the main office and not to your child directly.

- Without much discussion, walk your child to the playground or wherever children have to line up to go into the school building.

Do this about 5 minutes before your child is expected to enter the school building. Ignore whining, crying, minor physical complaints, and statements or questions about wanting to go home or not be in school.

- Say final goodbyes and give your child a hug. Even if he is crying or clingy, praise him for being brave and going to school. Remember, you always want to get across your point that school attendance is expected.

- Arrange to have a friendly school official (preferably one known and liked by your child) come outside or stand in the school doorway to greet your child, smile, and escort him to class.

- Leave quickly.

Do not allow your child to come with you to the car and do not drive your child back home. If for some reason you absolutely cannot get your child into the school building on time, stay there as long as necessary, even a couple of hours, to get your child to eventually go into the school building. It is far better for your child (and for you tomorrow) to enter school at 10:30 and stay the rest of the day than to miss the entire day of school and be home. Remember also to punish any delays going to school later that evening.

I know this can be hard to do. My guess, though, is that your child will be upset for a few minutes inside the school building and then be fine for the rest of the school day. When I drop off my daughter at preschool, she sometimes cries. This makes me feel bad, of course, until I go to work, access the online webcam to her classroom, and see that she is having great fun! My experience working with young children with school refusal behavior over the years has also shown this to be generally true.

If you are worried, then you may wish to contact your child's teacher or guidance counselor later that morning to see how your child is doing and to ease your concerns about his mood. If you discover that your child is still crying at lunchtime and beyond, then you may wish to try some of the methods covered in chapter 3. If your child goes to school and sobs continually for the entire day, then you may wish seek the help of a qualified mental health professional (see chapter 1). In general, though, the more you practice this entering-school routine and the more you tell your child that you expect him to go to school, the easier it will be for him to enter school.

Forcing a Child to Attend School

What if you cannot get your child out of the house to even try the entering-school routine at the playground? Parents often ask me in this situation: should I just force my child to go to school? Forcing a child to go to school can be tricky, so I generally do not recommend it except under very specific circumstances. My preference is to set up the morning routine, apply the rewards and punishments, and tell your child that you expect him to go to school. Allow these methods to take their course for at least a few weeks before moving on to something more drastic like forced school attendance.

If you have a particularly willful child who absolutely refuses to leave the house or car, then you might consider forcibly taking him to school. However, I recommend doing so only as a last resort and under all of the following conditions:

- Your child is not older than age 10 years.

- Your child has no distress whatsoever about school (see chapters 3 and 4).

- Your child is refusing school *only* for attention from you.

- Your child fully understands what will happen if he does not leave home or the car.

- Your child is missing more school days than he goes.

- Two adults can take your child to school *every day*.

- School officials have been notified of your plan and have agreed to meet you at your car or the entrance to the school building to escort your child to class.

- You have no guilt, distress, hesitation, or reservations about doing this.

- You have the energy and ability to do this.

If any of these do not apply to your situation, then I do not recommend forced school attendance. Should you try this approach, however, this is what I do recommend at the end of the morning routine:

- Tell your child in advance that you will physically take him to school if he refuses to leave home or the car. If your child does start to refuse to do so, give one warning: "Go now or we will take you there."

- If necessary, have two adults (possibly including yourself) carry your child to the car and place him in the backseat with another adult who can sit with him and prevent him from leaving the car. Do not do this on your own!

- Drive your child to school and ignore crying, tantrums, and other disruptive school refusal behaviors. Stay calm, neutral, and matter-of-fact in your tone of voice. In this situation, it is usually best not to say anything at all.

- Bring your child to the school entrance where a school official can meet him and escort him to class. Leave quickly and do not worry about saying goodbye or exchanging hugs if your child is throwing a temper tantrum.

- Contact school officials later that morning to see what happened once you left. Be sure to punish your child's morning disruptive behavior later that evening.

If you are unsure about using this method, then do not do it. I have found that forced school attendance can very effective, but the danger is that parents will hesitate or give up on doing it. If this happens, a child's school refusal behavior is greatly reinforced and it will be much harder for him to go back to school later. If you have a particularly difficult situation and are not sure about forcing your child to go to school, then use the other methods described in this chapter, consult with school officials about your options (see next section), or consult with a qualified mental health professional (see chapter 1).

Missing Most of the School Day

If your child is missing most or all of the school day, then the first step toward full-time school attendance should be small. Ask your child what

My Child Is Home From School: What Now?

If your child is home from school because it was impossible to get him in the school building, then be sure to have him sit in a chair or on his bed for most of the school day. If you had to take your child to work, then have him sit in one spot. *Wherever your child is, be sure that he is in a rather dull place and does not have access to fun things such as television and video games or the telephone and computer. In addition, keep your verbal and physical attention toward your child to a minimum.* Children who refuse school for attention want your attention. If they do not get much of your attention for missing school, then they will be less likely to refuse school.

If your child is at home or your workplace during the day, then have him complete schoolwork or do other academic tasks such as reading textbooks, finishing worksheets, and writing essays. If others are watching your child, ask them to try to follow these recommendations. Following the end of normal school hours, say after 3 p.m., *do not let your child off the hook.* Instead, have him do chores or stay in his room; do not allow your child to socialize. In addition, any punishments that you have set up for school refusal behavior can be carried out in the evening. If your child missed most of the school week, then restrictions and punishments can be carried out on the weekends.

Although this approach may sound harsh, the goal is to deprive your child of attention when he is refusing school and to lavish attention when he does go to school. When your child does go to school, be sure to give praise and more formal rewards and remind your child that this is the kind of behavior you like to see.

time of day is easiest for him to go to school. Younger children often tell me that they would go to school if school lasted only a couple of hours. So I tell them: go to school for a couple of hours! Find out what time of day your child is willing to go to school and use that as a starting point. Then you can gradually increase the amount of time your child spends in school.

If your child is missing most or all of the school day, then first pursuing a part-time schedule is a good idea. As mentioned in chapter 3, the first step in a part-time schedule can involve one of the following:

- Your child goes to school in the morning and is then allowed to come home within an hour (then you gradually work forward by adding more time).

- Your child goes to school at 2 p.m. and is then allowed to come home when school normally ends, say at 3:10 (then you gradually work backward by adding more time).

- Your child goes to school only for lunch and is then allowed to come home afterward (then you gradually add more school time before and after lunch).

- Your child goes to school only for his favorite class or time of day (then you gradually add more classes or school time).

- Your child attends a school room other than his classroom, such as the school library, guidance counselor or nurse's office, or main lobby (then gradually add more classroom time).

Because I covered these steps at length in chapter 3, I will not repeat myself here. However, if your child is missing most of the school day, then I invite you to read chapter 3 and, in particular, the section on changing the "doing" part of distress. This section will give you more detailed ideas about how to set up a part-time attendance schedule that will eventually lead to full-time attendance. Be sure that you continue to practice all of the methods described in this chapter, including setting up the morning routine and giving rewards, punishments, and good commands. Even if your child is not currently going to school, then I encourage you to continue with the morning routine and practice other methods during the day.

Do's and Don'ts!

I know that I have given you a lot of information in this chapter. Here is a list of some do and don't reminders.

Do:

- Set up a regular morning routine that allows plenty of time for everyone to get ready for school and work.

- Reward your child for properly getting ready in the morning and completing the morning routine.

- Punish your child for not completing the morning routine or for refusing to enter school.

- Give rewards and punishments in the morning and evening.

- Praise good behavior and ignore poor behavior.

- Expect your child to go to school each day.

- Work closely with school officials when developing your morning plan.

- Speak to your child in a calm, matter-of-fact tone and give brief commands.

- Limit phone calls and statements and questions about going to school.

- Set up a plan to deal with running away from the school campus.

- Seek support from others, especially for the morning routine.

- Pursue a part-time school attendance schedule if necessary.

- Be consistent and use these methods every day.

Don't:

- Fight, yell, lecture, criticize, negotiate, beg, or bribe your child to go to school.

- Dance to your child's tune.

- Stay with your child at school.

- Linger at school or the playground when your child is supposed to enter school.

- Allow your child to come home early.

- Visit your child at school during the day.

- Use forced school attendance unless all of the conditions mentioned earlier apply.

▪ Final Comments

Dealing with children who refuse school for attention takes a lot of work and patience. You will find yourself truly tested during those mornings when you are trying to ignore poor behavior, tune out the screaming, and put aside your own doubts and guilt. Be sure to get help from other people if you need it. But the most important thing to remember is to *be consistent and persistent!* The more you try these methods *every day*, even if it takes a few weeks, the more likely you will see your child more easily go to school. Hang in there! You can do it!

Children Who Refuse School to Do Fun Things Outside School

Maya is a 16-year-old girl who has been skipping afternoon classes to hang out with her friends outside of school. Although Maya does go to school in the morning, she often meets up with her friends Callie and Nita in the middle of the day for lunch. Many times the teens eat lunch off the school campus and then "ditch" the rest of the day to go to a local mall or spend time at Callie's house. Maya is not distressed about school but complains sometimes that school is boring. She tried to hide her absences from her parents, but the principal recently informed Maya's mother that her daughter has now missed at least seven afternoons of school.

This chapter will be *more helpful* to you if your child matches Maya's situation or if one or more of the following is true:

- Your child is refusing school *only* to get to do more fun things outside of school.

- Your child is skipping class to be with friends or to do other fun things.

- Your child prefers to sleep in during the morning instead of going to school.

This chapter will be *less helpful* to you if one or more of the following is true:

- Your child is refusing school *only* because she is very distressed about something related to school (see chapter 3).

- Your child is refusing school *only* because she is very distressed about social or performance situations at school (see chapter 4).

- Your child is refusing school *only* for attention from you or a significant other (see chapter 5).

Children Who Do Fun or Dangerous Things Instead of School

In chapter 2 we discussed different reasons why children have trouble going to school. One reason is that some children, like Maya, enjoy doing more fun activities outside of school. In Maya's case, for example, she enjoyed hanging out with her friends and spending time at another's house. Other kids who refuse school do so because they enjoy sleeping late, watching television, riding their bicycle, and shopping, among other things. In some cases, these kids refuse school to do more dangerous things such as use drugs, shoplift, or destroy property.

Children who refuse school to do more fun things outside of school are often older and try to keep their absences secret. These kids may or may not show acting-out behavior problems, but they do often fight with their parents and others so that their absences can continue. After all, they like doing what they are doing! Maya, for example, greatly enjoyed her time with friends and did not want that time to end. However, she and her mother had intense arguments about the value of an education and about going to school. Maya's mother insisted that her daughter go to school, but Maya found school to be "stupid" and did not see the point of even graduating. Instead, she was greatly tempted by her friend's offers to leave school and have fun.

Many of these children are *not particularly distressed* about school. If you feel that your child *is* distressed about school, then be sure to read chapters 3 and 4. In addition, many of these children do not seek attention for their school refusal behavior. On the contrary, they usually like their absences to be well-kept secrets. If you feel your child does seek your attention when missing school, then be sure to read chapter 5.

To change your child's outlook about going to school and to help improve her school attendance, I will concentrate on the following:

- Monitoring your child

- Setting up regular meetings with your child

- Setting up written contracts for getting ready for school and for going to school

- Escorting your child from class to class

- Knowing what to say to friends who want your child to leave school

- Changing what you say to your child

Why Am I Doing This?

If your child resembles Maya, my guess is that she is quite good at slipping away from school and spending time with friends, coming home to watch television or play video games, or failing to show up at school to wander about. You may be particularly frustrated and confused about this secretive behavior and may even be angry at school officials for not watching your child more closely or for delays in letting you know what's been going on. All of this is understandable.

We have to change some things in this situation. First, we must make sure that you or school officials (or both) know *exactly where your child is at all times of the day*. This does not mean grounding your child for the rest of her life, of course, but it does mean keeping a very close eye on her whereabouts and school attendance. This will require a lot of cooperation between you and school officials, so I encourage you to set aside any friction or irritation you might have with anyone at your child's school. What we need to develop is a regular system of communication and watchfulness so that your child is less able to slip out of school.

Another thing we have to change is all the fun things your child gets to do when she is out of school. Right now your child gets a lot of rewards for being out of school and perhaps very little reward for being in school. This is kind of normal: many of us take our child's school attendance for granted and tend to pay little attention to it until the attendance becomes a problem. Because your child is having trouble staying in school, however, this needs to change. We have to set up a situation where your child is getting some reward for going to school and is receiving some punishment for not going to school. Many older kids prefer rewards that they can touch and see, so these are the ones we will concentrate on in this chapter.

I know what you might be thinking: But my kid should be going to school anyway without special rewards! I agree. But please keep some things in mind. First, your child is having trouble staying in school, and this has to change fast. Second, I will not be recommending that you reward your child *directly* for school attendance. For example, I do not suggest paying a child to go to school. Instead, I prefer *indirect* methods. For example, a child might be expected to go to school to earn the privilege of being allowed to do a certain chore at home for which she may be paid. Third, we will be setting up punishments as well for not going to school.

In some cases, setting up these rewards and punishments is not enough. In tougher cases like Maya's, parents or others must sometimes escort a child from class to class so that she can receive rewards for school attendance. I know this sounds like a difficult thing to do, and it is, but I will discuss different ways of doing this that do not necessarily mean you have to be at school.

Kids who refuse school to do more fun things outside of school, like Maya, often have another issue that we will also have to deal with. Many of these kids have friends or acquaintances that often tempt them to ditch school. In Maya's case, for example, she rarely left school on her own but did so after her friends encouraged her to skip classes. This is a special problem because we can often get kids to go to school but cannot control what their friends say to them there. However, we can change what your child says and does to refuse offers to miss school and attend class. So, I will make some suggestions about what your child can do and say to turn down offers to miss school.

Finally, my guess is that you and your child have been fighting a lot about school attendance. Again, this is understandable, given how frustrating this behavior can be. So, I will make some suggestions as well about how you and your child can reach a reasonable agreement about school attendance and your child's activities outside of school.

All of these recommendations will require a lot of effort on your part. The methods in this chapter will be helpful *only* if you and/or your spouse/partner:

- Have the *will and the ability* to carry out the methods

- Support each other

- Are confident that your child is refusing school *only* to do more fun things outside of school

- Are working closely with school officials (no fighting with them!)

- Can commit to doing the methods consistently and permanently

- Have a fairly good relationship with your child

A reminder: Some kids refuse school because the school climate is quite boring and unchallenging. In this case, a child may simply want to stay home and play on the computer all day. More kids might not refuse school if only school were a little more interesting! This situation is a little different than what I have described so far—a child who is refusing school mostly to get to do *a lot of fun things outside of school*. If your daughter is refusing school because she says school is "boring" and she is not leaving school mostly to be with friends, then work closely with school officials to see if class schedule changes, enrollment in extracurricular activities, or increased time with friends at school might help increase her school attendance.

Monitoring Your Child

Because children who skip school to do more fun things outside of school are usually secretive about their behavior, parents are often shocked to learn that their child has been skipping school. Once you have discovered this problem, though, you must work hard to make sure you know where your child is *at all times of the day* and not just during school hours. If your child is starting to leave the school campus, for example, we want to make sure we catch this as quickly as possible so she does not miss a large part of the school day.

How can we do this? I have several suggestions:

- Meet with your child's teachers, guidance counselor, and other relevant school officials to make sure you are informed *immediately* when your child has skipped school. Some schools are able to "keep an eye" on a particular child and others are not. At a minimum, however, you want to know *as soon as possible* if your child has missed a class.

- If school officials say they can "keep an eye" on your child, try to set up a system whereby someone is watching your child during times *when she is most likely* to leave the school campus. Often this occurs after lunch, but your child may leave school at certain times in the morning or afternoon as well. If your child is seen leaving the school campus, then she can be brought back into school (and suffer consequences such as detention as a result). If you do not know when your child usually leaves school, or if your child leaves school at different times of the day, then try to make sure she is monitored as much as possible throughout the day.

- Ask your child to call you or contact a school official during a time at school when she is often absent. Many kids such as Maya are absent in the afternoon, so you may require your child to visit the guidance counselor's office at 1 and 2 to make sure she is actually in school. If she does not show up at these times, you should be told right away. If your child leaves at different times of the school day, then she can check in with you or a school official once per hour.

- Require that your child keep an "attendance log" that is signed by each teacher. Your child should get each teacher's signature to show that she was in class and then show you this log each night. Work with school officials to set this up. A sample attendance log is provided here (worksheet 6.1). Feel free to photocopy this worksheet as much as you need or download multiple copies from the companion Web site at www.oup.com/us/schoolrefusal. A good rule of thumb is that a lack of signature (for whatever reason) is the same as a missed class. Do not accept any excuses for a missed signature.

- As much as possible, find out where your child is likely to go when out of school. Many kids pick the same spot, but others roam around. Get names, addresses, telephone numbers, and other information about where your child is likely to be if not in school. This will help you find your child more quickly if necessary. *If you know your child has left the school campus, then find her and bring her back to school if during school hours or home if after school hours.* It is very important that you try to deprive your child of the ability to do fun things outside of school during school hours.

Class (starting with 1st period)   *Teacher's name*   *Teacher's signature and date*

_____   _____   _____

_____   _____   _____

_____   _____   _____

_____   _____   _____

_____   _____   _____

_____   _____   _____

_____   _____   _____

Be in the practice of knowing where your child is *even during non-school hours.* For example, always require your child to check in with you when out with friends and get names, addresses, and telephone numbers of places where your child plans to be. If your child does not check in with you at set times, say every hour or so, then find her and bring her home. Also, set a curfew that is very early on school nights and perhaps a bit later on Friday and Saturday nights.

The most important thing to remember is that you should know at all times where your child is and, if you do not know, to find her and to bring her to school or home. I know this requires a lot of effort on your part. Therefore, I strongly encourage you to talk to others who can help locate your child and bring her to school or home. Enlist the help of school officials, grandparents and other relatives, friends, and neighbors. Also, stay in close contact with the parents of your child's friends. Get to know them well and try to set up a system where you are called immediately if your child goes somewhere she is not supposed to be. *If your child expects to be closely watched at all times, especially at school, and knows she will be sought and found if she skips school, then she will be less likely to leave school.* Be an eagle-eye, a bloodhound, and a retriever!

Setting Up Regular Meetings With Your Child

Later in this chapter I will be asking you to negotiate solutions to your child's problems getting ready for school and going to school. To do this, though, you must have regular meetings with your child to discuss school preparation and attendance and what can be done to improve school preparation and attendance. I recommend that you meet with your child once per night for at least a few minutes. Ask for the attendance log if you have asked her to complete one. In addition, talk about what happened at

> You must have regular meetings with your child to discuss school preparation and attendance.

school that day, what homework she has, what problems came up that day, and whether she was tempted to miss school.

Try to make these meetings as stress-free as possible. I know this may be tough, given how upset you might be about school absences. But keep in mind that your goal is to support your child and her attempts to go to school. You may have discovered at this point that lecturing, criticizing, demanding, yelling, and physical punishment do not work. Instead, you will have to negotiate solutions to different problems *with your teenager.* Let your child know: "I'm willing to work with you to give you what you want (such as time with friends) *as long as* you work with me to give me what I want (such as school attendance)." In addition, let you child know that you will help her deal with problems related to school attendance, such as the mounds of make-up work that may be due. All of these problems are fixable if you and your child work together and if you seek the help of relevant school officials.

Contracts for School Preparation and Attendance

When children become teenagers, parents find it harder to simply tell their kids what to do. Teenagers are growing up quickly and often want to be adults as fast as possible! This means reaching for independence in different ways. This is normal, and many parents allow their teenagers more freedom than their younger kids. For example, a teenager might be allowed to spend time with friends at a mall, begin dating, and start driving a car. On the other hand, some teenagers want a little too much independence and end up doing things like skipping school. So, we have to find a good balance of what your teenager wants to do and what she is allowed to do.

Another thing that parents do differently with teenagers than younger kids is to *negotiate solutions to problems.* You might be able to simply order a 7-year-old to clean her room, but trying the same thing with a 17-year-old is often not useful; in fact, doing so can lead to a lot of yelling and fighting and stress. What many parents find is that they have to *work out some agreement* with their teenagers. For example, a parent and teenage girl might agree that, in exchange for keeping her room clean, the teenager can go out with her friends on Friday night under certain conditions (such as being home by 11 p.m., calling home every hour, letting parents know of any change in plans).

A teenager who is skipping school should be dealt with in the same way. We must recognize that your teenager wants independence, and we must recognize that the best way to reduce school refusal behavior is to negotiate some kind of solution to the problem. I am not suggesting that you cave in to any outrageous demands from your child, of course. But I am suggesting that you try a method where you and your teenager can hammer out an agreement that gives her what she wants, such as some independence, but under certain conditions that you want, such as getting ready for school in the morning and staying in school for the entire day.

How can we do this? I recommend that you and your child develop *written contracts*, much like a lawyer would do. A contract is an agreement that you and your child work out together to make sure everyone gets what they want. Developing these contracts or agreements will take a lot of effort on your part and your child's part, and I recommend that they be part of the nightly discussion you have with your child (see earlier section).

What does a contract look like? We have provided a sample contract here. The contract should be kept simple at first and should include four things. First, a "privileges" column contains *the kinds of things your child wants*. I recommend that these privileges be things that your child can touch and see, such as time with friends, access to electronic equipment (computer, telephone, iPod, television), money, or special snacks or desserts. Allow only those privileges that fit within your family's value system. For example, if your child is overweight, then special snacks or desserts might not be the best reward. Or if your child wants expensive computer software, feel free to say that this is not affordable.

> *Allow only those privileges that fit within your family's value system.*

Second, a "responsibilities" column will contain *the kinds of things that you want*. The things you want should also be things that can be touched and seen, such as getting out of bed on time, getting ready for school, staying in school for an entire day, and completing chores around the house. Please understand that you should not "load your child up" with responsibilities right off the bat. Instead, we need to take things one step at a time.

Third, the contract contains places where you and your child, once you agree to the "privileges" and "responsibilities" of the contract, sign and date the contract. This helps make the contract "official" and makes the contract something you can rely on or point to instead of arguing or yelling. Let the contract and the fact that everyone signed it do your talking for you. If your child complains about going to school, for example, you can simply point to the contract!

The fourth part of a contract, general statements, is a section where privileges and responsibilities are made a little clearer (see section on step 1 of the contract).

Sample Contract

Privileges   *Responsibilities*

General statements

Everyone who signs this contract agrees to the conditions of this contract and to read and initial the contract every day.

Child's signature: _____

Parent's signature: _____

Date: _____

Working Together on a Contract

A contract is a written agreement that you and your child develop to help ease tension in the house and, ideally, to give everyone most of what they want. A contract *is not* a document that contains mostly what *one party* wants. If, for example, your child will not work with you on the contract, or has demands that are unreasonable, then something other than the contract will have to be tried (such as the other methods described in this chapter and in other chapters). On the other hand, if you are making so many demands of your child that she does not even want to participate, or feels that her input is not valued, then the contract process will not work either. Some give-and-take on your part and your child's part is needed for contracts to be successful.

During your discussions with your child, ask her to write down a list of things that she wants. Note that I did not say a list of things she wants in return for going to school. Instead, she should give you a list of things that she would enjoy doing in general and that you can use as "bargaining chips" for the contract. Likewise, you should write down a list of things that you want. I recommend that you keep this list simple and *stick to three main topics*: a basic chore such as taking out the garbage, getting ready for school on time in the morning, and staying in school for an entire day. If you and your child become especially good at using contracts once school attendance is taken care of, then you can start tackling other issues of disagreement.

Once you have these lists, be sure that you and your child review each one. Take any item off the list that is unreasonable, such as going to school only 3 out of every 5 days! Make it clear to your child that she is expected to get ready for school and stay in school the entire day, but that you are willing to make sure that she will get some of what she wants if she does this. Once you have your final lists set, you are ready to try your first contract. Let's go to step 1.

Step 1: A Simple Contract

Your first contract with your child should be a *simple one* and one that you think is going to be successful. For example, you and your child may agree on one household chore. Your child could agree to take out the garbage on Tuesday and Friday and you could agree that, if she does, she can go out with friends under certain conditions on Friday night. You and your child must also agree, however, about what will happen if the garbage is *not taken out* on Tuesday or Friday. In this case, you could agree that your child will be grounded Friday night. *Do not start with a complicated contract!*

If you and your child reach an agreement like this, then the privileges and responsibilities could be formally written into a contract, such as the one

Nothing Motivates My Child!

Some parents complain that nothing motivates their child: "I've taken away everything from her and she still won't go to school!" Some kids are extremely willful and stubborn and seem not to care about any punishments (or even rewards) that you give. Trust me, though, they care. If you are in this situation, then you might want to meet with your child and set up a "clean slate." That is, start from scratch and get your child's input about what it will take for her to go back to school at least part of the time. I am not asking you to be held hostage to your child's demands. You want to make sure that you and your child are both asking for something reasonable. A good place to start is with a part-time school attendance schedule or attendance at an alternative educational placement such as a vocational school.

Give your child some basic access to things that she enjoys. This might include 30 minutes of television per day, 30 minutes of computer time per day, or a night with friends. Be clear that you are giving these things as part of a "good-faith" agreement that your child will try to go to school part-time. Then, as you develop a contract, you can take away these things if your child did not fulfill her end of the contract.

Even when nothing seems to motivate a child, the child must be doing something! Even if every electronic thing is taken away, kids often have access to books, cars, toys, discussions with their friends, junk foods, or other basic things. These are bargaining chips, so use them in a contract! Most kids will eventually try to go to school if the only thing they are allowed to do is sit on their beds! Still, if you find yourself at an impasse with your child, then seek out a qualified mental health professional (see chapter 1).

in figure 6.1. As you write out the contract, be sure that you and your child *go over every word* to make sure there are no misunderstandings. Ask your child if she has questions or changes, and make changes if necessary.

Also, be very specific about each statement that is in a contract. If necessary, write down what time the garbage should be taken out and who will check to make sure the garbage was taken out. Statements that help make a contract clearer can be written in the "general statements" section. No loopholes! Teenagers can be fantastic at taking advantage of weaknesses in a contract.

Figure 6.1
Sample first contract (household chore)

Privileges	Responsibilities
For the privilege of going out with her friends on Friday night,	Maya agrees to take out the garbage on Tuesday before 7 p.m. and on Friday before 7 p.m.

General statements

Should Maya not complete this duty on Tuesday or Friday, then she will be grounded Friday night.

Mom will check at 7 p.m. on Tuesday and Friday to make sure the garbage was taken out.

Maya must be home on Friday night by 11, be with Callie and Nita only at the mall, and call home every hour to check in.

This contract is good only for this week.

Everyone who signs this contract agrees to the conditions of this contract and to read and initial the contract every day.

Child's signature: _____

Parent's/parents' signature(s): _____

Date: _____

Be sure that you and your child are completely comfortable with every word of the contract and the contract itself. One thing you don't want is for your child to quickly agree to the contract just so she can leave the table and go watch television. Similarly, do not complete the contract if you feel *you* cannot follow through with its conditions. Do not make promises you cannot keep. Instead, make sure that you and your child fully agree with the wording of the contract and *encourage your child not to sign the contract until she feels the contract is completely fair.* Once everyone feels the contract is completely fair, however, then everyone should sign the contract at the bottom.

Also, be sure that every contract you develop, including this one, has a short timeline of no more than 1 week. The sample contract in figure 6.2, for example, could be tried for 5 days (Monday to Friday of a certain week) and expire after Friday. This allows you and your child to see what went right and what went wrong and to make changes to the contract as needed.

Now you are ready to put the contract into action and see what happens. One of three things is likely to happen:

- The contract worked well: the garbage was taken out and your child had a fun night with her friends on Friday night! The best possible scenario!

- Someone did not fulfill her end of the contract: either the garbage was not taken out (so grounding on Friday night should occur) or the garbage was taken out but your child was not allowed to go out on Friday night (in which case, shame on you!).

- The contract was forgotten or did not work for some reason.

Let's talk about each of these separately. If the contract worked, great! Be sure to praise your child (and yourself) for agreeing to do something and following through on the agreement. If this happened, sit down with your child and say how glad you are that you and she were able to negotiate a solution to a problem. This is much better than arguing, so good job! I recommend two things at this point. First, extend this first contract to another Monday-to-Friday period or whatever week you choose. Second, go to step 2 (see later section).

If someone did not fulfill her end of the contract, find out why. For example, why was the garbage not taken out? Did your child forget? Was the task too hard? Did she simply not care about the contract or about going out Friday night? Do not have this discussion until the contract is officially over. Do not, for example, nag your child to take out the garbage on the day she is supposed to do so—*let the contract and its conditions do your talking for you!* Watch your own behavior as well; be sure to follow through on any contract rewards that are due your child. If you promised a Friday night out, and she earned it, then give her a Friday night out!

In this situation, try to rework the contract so your child is able to receive its rewards. For example, you may have to make the contract or the task simpler and easier to remember. Or you may have to "tweak" or increase the rewards and punishments to make them more effective. Also, some children fail the first contract because they are testing their parents: will Mom let me go out anyway even though I didn't take out the garbage? If this is the case, stick to your guns and to the contract! If your child did not do what she agreed to do, then go ahead with the consequences (grounding in this case). If your child is willing to try the contract or some simpler contract again, then go ahead and do so. If your child is unwilling to try writing another contract, then you may wish to use the other methods described in this chapter and in other chapters.

Finally, the contract may have been forgotten or did not work for some reason. We lead very busy lives, and so the contract may have gotten pushed to the side. I recommend in this case that you and your child read and initial the contract *every day* to remind yourselves of its privileges and responsibilities. Post the contract on the refrigerator door so that it is plain to see. Also, find out why the contract did not work and write a new one that has a better chance of working. *Contracts will work only if they are taken very seriously and made a top priority!*

Once you have some success with this first, simple contract, then go to step 2. If you are having trouble with the first contract, then continue writing contracts that involve small tasks like chores. You want to be sure that this first contract goes well before tackling more difficult problems such as school preparation and attendance. In the meantime, however, work closely with school officials regarding the other methods in this chapter. One thing you don't want is too long a delay getting your child to attend school full-time.

Step 2: Getting Ready for School

If your first contract went well and you and your child have agreed to continue with this method, then the next step involves getting ready for school. If your child has no problems getting ready for school, then you can jump ahead to step 3 (see next section). If your child has trouble getting out of bed or other problems getting ready in the morning, however,

Problems Getting Out of Bed

Some teenagers miss school because they have a lot of trouble getting out of bed in the morning. Teenagers do need a lot of sleep because their bodies are changing, but they still have to get up in the morning and go to school! If your child has this problem, then be sure she is getting plenty of sleep. The following will help:

■ Make sure your child only sleeps in her bed and does not use it for other activities such as reading, watching television, calling people, or completing homework.

■ Be sure your child is in bed *with lights out* at an early time, say 8 to 9 hours before having to get up.

■ Avoid caffeine, nicotine, alcohol, and exercise before bedtime.

■ Practice relaxation methods close to bedtime (see chapter 3).

■ Follow the same routine before bedtime and begin this routine 30 minutes before lights out.

■ Set curfew for at least 2 hours before bedtime.

■ Speak to your pediatrician about sleep medication if necessary.

What should you do if you cannot get your child out of bed? Some parents like to do drastic things such as pour cold water on the bed or bang pots and pans in the child's bedroom. I am not a big fan of these methods. However, I do encourage you to get up very early and wake your child in stages, much like a snooze alarm. If your child has to be up by 6 a.m., for example, get up at 5:15 a.m. and wake your child at 5:30, 5:40, 5:50, 5:55, and 5:59 a.m. Tell your child how many minutes she has left before having to get up. Set a loud alarm as well across the room. If your child still won't get up, then continue to speak to her every 5 minutes, and do make sleeping a difficult thing to do. Also, set up contracts to give rewards and punishments for getting up or not getting up from bed. Finally, *do not give up and let your child sleep late and miss school completely.* If your child finally gets up and goes to school an hour late, this is better than missing most or all of the school day.

then this next contract step is for you. If there is great urgency about increasing your child's school attendance at this point, then steps 2 and 3 (see next section) may be combined.

Developing a contract at this second step involves the same ideas I discussed in the previous section: meeting with your teenager, being specific

Figure 6.2
Sample Second Contract (school preparation: getting out of bed only)

Privileges	Responsibilities
For the privilege of staying up until 10 p.m on a particular night,	*Maya agrees to rise from bed no later than 6:50 a.m. that morning.*

General statements

If Maya does not rise from bed by 6:50 a.m., she must go to bed that evening at 8:30 p.m.

Rising from bed means that Maya's entire body is out of bed by 6:50 a.m.

Mom will make sure Maya's alarm is set and that she wakes Maya by 6:40 a.m.

This contract is good only for this week (Monday–Friday).

Everyone who signs this contract agrees to the conditions of this contract and to read and initial the contract every day.

Child's signature: _____

Parent's/parents' signature(s): _____

Date: _____

about what you and she want, keeping the timeline of the contract short, and coming up with a final agreement. A contract at this point might be very simple. For example, you may agree with your daughter that she has to be out of bed by a certain time in the morning. If she does, then some good thing happens; if she does not, then some less-than-good thing happens. See figure 6.2 for an example.

If your child has a lot of trouble getting ready for school in the morning, and not just getting out of bed, then you can build a morning routine into the contract. The morning routine could be very similar to what I discussed in chapter 5. For example:

6:50 a.m.   Rise from bed

6:50–7 a.m.   Go to the bathroom and wash (10 minutes)

7–7:20 a.m.   Eat breakfast (which should be ready by 7 or whenever breakfast time starts) (20 minutes)

7:20–7:30 a.m.   Brush teeth in bathroom and wash as needed (10 minutes)

7:30–7:50 a.m.   Dress and accessorize for school (20 minutes)

7:45–8 a.m.   Make final preparations for school such as putting on a jacket or getting backpack ready) (15 minutes)

8–8:20 a.m.   Extra time (if child is ready, she can do what she wants inside the house; if child is not ready, she can use this time to finish) (20 minutes)

8:20–8:50 a.m.   Commute to school and child enters school (30 minutes)

Again, negotiate this morning routine with your teenager (this is different with younger kids and what I said in chapter 5, where I encourage parents to simply tell their younger child what will happen in the morning). When you develop the contract, keep it simple. I do not recommend setting up privileges and responsibilities for each step of the morning routine. Instead, use this routine as a "guide" or "roadmap" and set up privileges and responsibilities for being ready for school on time (figure 6.3).

Once you have developed this contract, put the contract into action and see what happens. As I mentioned before, let the contract run its course and do not nag your child to get ready in the morning. Simply give the consequences spelled out in the contract if she fails to complete the morning routine. This may take some patience and persistence on your part and your child's part. Sometimes this step can take a few weeks.

If the contract is not working after a couple of weeks and your child is still unable to rise from bed or get ready on time, then try to rework the

Figure 6.3
Sample Second Contract (school preparation: completing the morning routine)

Privileges	Responsibilities
For the privilege of staying up until 10 p.m. on a particular night,	Maya agrees to rise from bed no later than 6:50 a.m. that morning.
For the privilege of having access to television and the computer that evening,	Maya agrees to complete the morning routine by 8:20 a.m.
For the privilege of having access to television, the computer, and her iPod and telephone that evening,	Maya agrees to complete the morning routine by 8 a.m.

General statements

If Maya does not rise from bed by 6:50 a.m., she must go to bed that evening at 8:30 p.m.

Rising from bed means that Maya's entire body is out of bed by 6:50 a.m.

Mom will make sure Maya's alarm is set and that she wakes Maya by 6:40 a.m.

Mom will decide what time Maya is ready in the morning. Mom and Maya can discuss whether Maya is done (and what else needs to be done) at 7:50 a.m. and 8:10 a.m. to give Maya a good chance of being done by 8 or 8:20.

If Maya is not ready by 8 a.m., she loses access to television and the computer that evening.

If Maya is not ready by 8:20 a.m., she loses access to television, the computer, and her iPod and telephone that evening.

This contract is good only for this week (Monday–Friday).

Everyone who signs this contract agrees to the conditions of this contract and to read and initial the contract every day.

Child's signature: _____

Parent's/parents' signature(s): _____

Date: _____

contract so that it is simpler and easier to for your child to do. Or you may have to "tweak" or increase the rewards and punishments to make them more effective. Be firm in your expectation that your child should be getting ready for school, but recognize as well that changes might have to be made so she is able to receive the rewards in the contract.

For example, if your child can finally be ready by 10 a.m. and then go to school, start at this point for the contract and give contract rewards for being in school by 10 a.m. As she is able to be in school by 10, she can later be expected to be ready for school at gradually earlier times, such as 9:45, 9:15, and 8:45. These earlier times can be part of new contracts. A child who is getting ready for school and going to school for at least some of the day is preferable to a child who cannot get ready at an early time, loses all contract rewards as a result, and then will not even go to school. *Be flexible in your thinking when writing contracts.* Once your child is able to rise from bed and get ready for school, then you may be ready for the third and last step, which involves improved school attendance (see next section).

Step 3: School Attendance

Contracts for improving your child's school attendance should involve all the recommendations I made earlier for steps 1 and 2. Again, negotiate the contract with your child, rework the contract (and its rewards and punishments) as necessary, keep the contract simple, use a short timeline, and let the contract do your talking for you. If your child is skipping only part of a school day or a class or two, then your first school attendance contract could require your child to stay in school the entire day (figure 6.4).

If your child is missing most or all of the school day, then the first school attendance contract should involve some *small step* toward full-time school attendance. In other words, you can start with a part-time schedule and go from there. Ask your child what time of day is easiest for her to go to school. Teenagers such as Maya often tell me they would go to school if school were held only in the morning. So I tell them: go to school for the morning! Find out what time of day your child is willing to go to school and use that as a starting point. Then, using the contracts, you can gradually increase the amount of time your child spends in school.

Figure 6.4
Sample Third Contract (school attendance)

Privileges	Responsibilities
For the privilege of seeing her friends on the weekend,	Maya agrees to have no more than zero marked absences this week.
For the privilege of being paid $10 for vacuuming the house on Saturday,	Maya agrees to have no more than one marked class absence this week
For the privilege of being paid $5 for vacuuming the house on Saturday,	Maya agrees to have no more than two marked class absences this week.

General statements

A marked absence is equal to one missed class and is determined by the school.

"Vacuuming the house" means vacuuming the family room, living room, all bedrooms, and the stairs and landing. Mom will check to see that the vacuuming was done well.

If Maya has one or more marked absences this week, she may not see her friends this weekend.

If Maya has two or more marked absences this week, she must vacuum the house for free. If she does not vacuum the house, then she loses her computer, television, iPod, and telephone.

This contract is good only for this week (Monday–Friday).

Everyone who signs this contract agrees to the conditions of this contract and to read and initial the contract every day.

Child's signature: _____

Parent's/parents' signature(s): _____

Date: _____

NOTE: This contract may be done in addition to the other contracts mentioned so far.

If your child is missing most or all of the school day, then first pursuing a part-time schedule is a good idea. As mentioned in chapter 3, the first step in a part-time schedule can involve one of the following:

- Having your child go to school in the morning and be allowed to come home within an hour (then gradually working forward by adding more time)

- Having your child go to school at 2 p.m. and be allowed to come home when school normally ends, say at 3:10 (then gradually working backward by adding more time)

- Having your child go to school only for lunch and be allowed to come home afterward (then gradually adding more school time before and after lunch)

- Having your child go to school only for her favorite class or time of day (then gradually adding more classes or school time)

- Having your child attend a school room other than her classroom, such as the school library, guidance counselor or nurse's office, or main lobby (then gradually adding more classroom time)

Because I covered these steps at length in chapter 3, I will not repeat myself here. However, if your child is missing most of the school day, then I invite you to read chapter 3 and, in particular, the section on changing the "doing" part of distress. This section will give you more detailed ideas about how to set up a part-time attendance schedule that will eventually lead to full-time attendance.

As you are doing this, however, be sure you continue to practice all of the methods described in this chapter, including setting up contracts and escorting a child from class to class (see next section). Even if your child is not currently going to school, then I encourage you to continue with the morning routine and practice other methods during the day (see chapter 5).

You may be facing a situation where your child has been out of school for some time, makeup work has piled sky-high, and your child is at high risk of failing the rest of the school year. Many kids ask me, "What is the point of going back to school if I can't get all the makeup work done or if I'm going to fail the school year anyway?"

These are legitimate questions: I wouldn't want to go to school either if I thought my situation was hopeless and school attendance was pointless. What should you do in this situation? I recommend that you speak to school officials about the possibility of setting up a "504 plan" or an "individualized education plan" (IEP). A 504 plan comes from a federal law that mandates school districts to accommodate students with some condition that interferes with their learning. Examples of interfering conditions include physical problems such as chronic medical illnesses or mental problems such as depression or anxiety or learning or attention-deficit/hyperactivity disorder. If your child might have one or more of these latter problems, seek an assessment and possible diagnosis from a qualified mental health professional (see chapter 1).

IEPs or 504 plans may be used to change class schedules, makeup work, credits, or other conditions that might make it easier for your child to attend school. If your child can go to school at least part-time, for example, and complete some schoolwork, then this could be built into the 504 plan. Be sure to work closely with school officials to see what your options are. If your child has a developmental disorder such as mental retardation, autism, or Asperger's disorder, then she may have an IEP. An IEP can also be designed to help youths return to school by changing class schedules and other key areas.

Escorting a Child From Class to Class

You may find that your child is willing to complete a school attendance contract but is still tempted to miss school and does continue to miss school. I certainly do not want you to be in a position where you are punishing your child all of the time. Instead, I want her to get rewards for going to school! If you find this is the case for you, then I recommend two things. One recommendation involves escorting your child from class to class. I will discuss this recommendation in this section. A second recommendation involves teaching your child how to turn down offers to miss school. I will discuss this recommendation in the next section.

Escorting your child from class to class is similar to the increased monitoring I discussed earlier. We must make sure that we know where your child is at all times. But we also want your child to get the rewards you set up for going to school. Even if your child is escorted from class to class, I count this as being in school. Therefore, your child is entitled to the rewards from the contract.

What exactly does "escorting from class to class" mean? Escorting can involve the following:

- Go to school with your child and physically walk her from one class to another. If you are willing and able do this *and* school officials agree to let you do this, then great. But I understand that many parents do not see this as a good option because they have to go to work and do other things.

- Ask someone you know to physically walk your child from class to class. Some relatives (grandparents especially), friends, or others have time during the day and could escort your child. Obviously this takes a lot of effort on the part of one person, so if different people could rotate doing the job, that would be great. But I understand that this option can be difficult to set up and maintain as well.

- Arrange with school officials to have someone at school escort your child from class to class. For example, a classmate, peer, or other child *whom you trust to do the right thing* could do the escorting and report to you or a school official any problems. In addition, on days your child misses school, this peer could call your child at night to encourage her to come to school the next day. Or a school official such as a guidance counselor or some other adult could do the escorting. The latter is sometimes tough to do, however, because of the drain on the school official's time.

- Arrange with school officials to have each teacher of each class walk your child to her next class. In this situation, your child's first-period teacher walks your child (at the end of first period) to her second-period class. The second-period teacher then walks your child (at the end of second period) to her third-period class, and so on for the rest of the day. This type of escorting has the advantage of not laying the burden on one person. In addition, your child could more easily get each teacher to sign her attendance log. A problem, of course, is that teachers or others may be overly busy and not always able to complete the escorting. See what can be arranged at your child's school.

A downside of escorting, of course, is that you or other people cannot escort your child forever. What will ideally happen, though, is that as your child receives contract rewards for being in school, the need for an escort should be less. If your child has been going to school for at least a couple of weeks with an escort, then you might be able to scale this back a little. For example, your child could be escorted in the morning but not the afternoon. Or she may be escorted only at "high-risk" times of the day such as around lunchtime but not other times of the day. If your child stays in school with a limited escort, then perhaps the escorting could end altogether. Even in this situation, however, remind your child that escorting can resume any time she decides to miss school again.

As you might guess, many kids do not like or want to be escorted from class to class. I agree that this can be quite embarrassing, which actually helps make the method more effective. If your child complains about the escort, tell her that sticking to the contract and staying in school will take away the escort. Your child has the choice of staying in school and receiving rewards for going to school, or missing school and having to be walked from class to class. Do not lecture, criticize, or yell. Simply tell your child that it is her choice as to what will happen (staying or not staying in school) and let the contract and the rewards and punishments do your talking for you.

■ *Refusing Offers to Miss School*

In addition to escorting, you may wish to help your child know what to do or say to refuse offers from others to miss school. In Maya's case, for example, she needed to know what she could do and say to Callie and Nita to turn down their offers to miss school. In addition, she needed to do this in a way that did not threaten her friendship with them but at the same time allowed her to stay in school.

I encourage teenagers to avoid situations at school that involve temptations to miss school. Find out from your child what these "high-risk" situations are for her. Many kids say, for example, that lunch (or right after lunch) is the time they are most likely to see friends who want them to miss school. If this is the case, then see if your child can eat lunch elsewhere or at another time of day. Be sure to consult with school officials to see what changes can be made. Other kids say that they are approached at their locker and then feel compelled to leave school. In this situation, see if you and your child can rearrange her locker visits to help avoid this.

What if your child is met with offers to miss school? In this case, give your child some suggestions for what she can say in this situation to turn down these offers. *Keep in mind that your child does not want to "lose face" in these situations.* She doesn't want to look foolish in front of her friends. In addition, making vague statements such as "I don't want to go" will not work well with peers who are persistent about ditching school.

Therefore, I recommend that you ask your child to blame other people, like you or teachers, for her need to stay in school. For example, you child may say, "My mom is on my case about staying the whole day," "My dad made me promise to stay in school this week or I can't hang out this week-end" (something from the contract, perhaps), or "My teachers are watching me like a hawk and I don't want detention." Or your child could tell her friends what big school projects are soon due, such as, "I can't; I've got that huge science project due Friday." Finally, if none of these seem to be working, your child could simply say, "Some other time," and walk away.

Silence is always a great conversation-killer!

Talk to your child *each day* about any offers she had to miss school and how she responded to these offers. Do not criticize or lecture or take over the conversation. Instead, remain supportive and help her develop ideas for doing or saying things differently to cut down on temptations to miss school.

> Talk to your child each day *about any offers she had to miss school and how she responded to these offers.*

If she did turn down an offer to miss school, give lots of praise! Also, work closely with school officials to see what could be done about minimizing your child's time with peers who tempt her to miss school.

■ Changing What You Say to Your Child

If you and your child are fighting a lot, I encourage you to use the methods in this chapter to try to negotiate solutions to different problems. Try to make a conscious effort to be patient and supportive while also firm and focused. Do not yell, nag, lecture, or criticize, as this will only make things worse. Also, as you are working with your child, avoid interrupting, name-calling, accusations, threats, insults, sarcasm, silence, and dwelling on past failures or problems. None of these actions will be productive, and they will serve only to drive your child away from the task of finding solutions to problems. *Instead, focus on the immediate future and what can be done right now!* Encourage your child to participate in the contract process, *listen carefully to what she has to say*, and praise her (and yourself) for good-faith attempts at solving difficult problems. You can do it!

On the other hand, you may find that your conflict with your child is so intense that it prevents you from using the contracts and other methods in this chapter. Some family members have such a long history of fighting that it is too difficult for them to try different ways of communicating on their own. In addition, some family members have gotten to the point of being so "fed up" with their child's behavior (and vice versa) that they are too frustrated and pessimistic to use the methods described in this chapter. If this is the case for you, then I recommend that you seek the help of a qualified mental health professional (see chapter 1).

■ Do's and Don'ts!

I know that I have given you a lot of information in this chapter. Here is a list of some do and don't reminders.

Do:

■ Keep very close tabs on your child during the day and evening—always know where she is!

■ Set up a system at school that helps prevent your child from leaving school.

Alternative School Placements

When older teenagers refuse school, their absences can reach a point where full-time school attendance in a regular classroom setting may not be possible or desirable. For other teenagers, the drudgery of high school is so overwhelming that they simply will not attend. For these teenagers, it may be useful to explore alternative educational placements.

Each school district is different, of course, so if you are considering an alternative educational placement, speak to knowledgeable school officials about where your child is eligible to go. Some school districts have part-time schools that meet only during mornings or evenings or weekends. Other alternatives include vocational schools, programs that involve home-based and school-based education, and summer classes. If your child is unwilling to attend regular school but is close to graduation, then attending one of these alternative settings may be the best option. The main goal is to make sure your child receives an adequate education and a high school diploma. How that is achieved, as long as it is achieved well, is less important than the fact that it *is* achieved.

- Have your child keep a regular attendance log.

- Set up regular nightly meetings with your child to discuss contracts, what happened at school that day, homework, problems, and offers to miss school.

- Develop contracts for household chores, school preparation, and school attendance.

- Find what rewards for going to school and punishments for not going to school work best.

- Escort your child from class to class if necessary so she can receive contract rewards.

- Work with your child and with school officials so your child can more easily avoid or turn down offers to miss school.

- Expect your child to go to school each day.

- Work closely with school officials when developing your plans.

- Speak to your child in a calm, matter-of-fact tone.

- Solve problems getting out of bed.

- Consider alternative educational placements where appropriate.

- Consider 504 and individualized education plans where appropriate.

- Contact the police when necessary.

- Be consistent and use the methods in this chapter every day.

Don't:

- Fight, yell, lecture, criticize, or physically punish your child to get her to go to school.

- Ignore your child's attendance problem during the day.

- Allow your child to do fun things outside of school during school hours.

- Forget any contract you have written.

- Forget to give rewards and punishments that are due your child.

Final Comments

Dealing with children who are older and who skip school to do fun things outside of school can be tough. I must warn you that solving this problem may take some time and will require a lot of effort on your part. As with any child with school refusal behavior, be sure to rely a lot on the help of others and work closely with school officials and other professionals if necessary.

Prevention and Special Circumstances

In previous chapters I covered ways of managing school refusal behavior in your child. In this chapter, I discuss:

- Preventing school refusal behavior in the future

- Special circumstances regarding your family or your child

- What to do if you have not found the methods in this book to be very helpful

- More technical information about the methods described in this book

Preventing School Refusal Behavior in the Future

If you helped your child return to school with little distress, congratulations! I am sure this required a lot of effort on your part, and you might be wondering: how do I keep it this way? Many parents are concerned about how to keep their child in school once he has gone back to school. This is a good concern. To help prevent school refusal behavior in the future, please keep the following suggestions in mind:

You must continue to practice whatever methods were helpful in getting your child back to school. Too many families assume that once the attendance crisis is over, things can go back to normal. Or parents just want to "leave well enough alone" and not discuss possible attendance problems. The problem with "going back to normal" is that this might mean going back to fighting, bribery, tension, and old ways of dealing with absenteeism! We don't want that. In addition, ignoring possible warning signs that school refusal behavior might happen again, or the "ostrich" approach of sticking one's head in the sand, is not a good strategy either. If you start to back off on what you did to get your child back in school, you have a good chance of having more problems in the future.

Instead, you must practice *every day* those methods that were successful in getting your child back to school. I know this is a lot of work, but the alternative, which means having to go through this all over again, is much worse and will cause you tremendous distress. In addition, you must constantly pay attention to any warning signs that might indicate another attendance problem. Examples include increased stress, physical complaints, statements about not wanting to go to school, and difficulty getting ready in the morning.

If your child was generally distressed about school, he should continue to practice methods of controlling physical "feelings" of distress and continue to attend school to manage these uncomfortable feelings. If your child was distressed about social and performance situations at school, he should continue to practice these methods of relaxation in addition to ways of thinking more realistically (the "STOP" method). If your child sought to miss school for your attention, you should continue to use the structured morning routine, rewards, punishments, and brief commands that I discussed. If your child sought to miss school to do more fun things outside of school, you should continue to monitor his whereabouts and attendance, develop contracts, escort him to school when necessary, and help him turn down offers to miss school.

I strongly recommend that you reread relevant sections of this book every once in a while. Pick which chapter or which section of the book seemed most relevant to you and bookmark it. Keep yourself and your child familiar with the methods that are needed to maintain good school attendance. Practice will not necessarily make perfect attendance, but good practice will help prevent serious problems from developing in the future.

Continue to keep track of your child's distress, morning behaviors, and attendance every day. I know it may be tempting to stop completing the worksheets, especially because of the busy lives we lead. What I have found, however, is that children who once had trouble going to school sometimes have additional trouble going to school later on. One way of reducing the chance of this happening is to constantly track your child's behavior. If your child knows that you are always watching him, then he will be less likely to miss school. Always know where your child is and, when necessary, have him complete a daily attendance log even when he is back to school full-time (see chapter 6). In addition, you may wish to have someone at school continue to keep an eye on your child during the day and let you know if any attendance problems occurred or nearly occurred.

Remain in close contact with relevant school officials throughout the school year. As I have mentioned several times during this book, a good working relationship with school officials is essential for returning a child to school and for preventing any problems in the future. Please continue to work with school officials so they can let you know immediately if your child has left school. Also, school officials can keep you informed about any other problems that might lead to more school refusal behavior. Examples of such problems include mood changes, social isolation, incomplete schoolwork, and disruptive behavior, among others. In addition, let school officials know immediately if *you* are having any new problems getting your child to school. That way, a new plan can be developed quickly to nip any problems in the bud.

You should also meet with school officials if you suspect that threats or school climate issues may be setting your child up for future attendance problems. Examples of threats include bullies or others who intimidate or terrorize students. Examples of school climate issues include poor teacher attitudes toward a child, inappropriate curriculum, an oppressive environment for diverse students, and difficult learning situations. If your child complains of these kinds of problems, then be sure to meet with school officials to seek solutions before school attendance becomes too difficult.

Meet with your child for at least 10 minutes each night to review the day at school. Do not let things pile up or get bottled up. Let your child vent about his school day, try to help him solve problems that might lead to future absences, help him practice the methods described in this book, and be supportive. If your child knows that you are willing to carve out at least a little bit of private time to discuss school issues, he will probably be more willing to work with you to help solve any problems that arise. And, if any legitimate problems do arise, make sure you discuss these issues with school officials as soon as possible. Do not allow any obstacles to school attendance to grow. Also, be sure to talk to your child about times he was most tempted to leave school and how he handled this situation.

Practice the methods in this book during breaks from school. Even during holiday breaks and summertime, make sure your child practices relaxation methods, socializes with other kids, stays on a regular morning routine, and gets enough sleep. In addition, do your part. Make sure, even during breaks, that you give appropriate rewards and punishments and good commands and always know where your child is and who he is spending time with. The more you use these methods, the more they become automatic or "second nature," which will help prevent future school refusal behavior.

Remind your child of the success he had going back to school. Occasionally tell your child how proud you are that he went back to school. *Never take your child's school attendance for granted!* In fact, you may even want to take pictures of accomplishments your child made when trying to go back to school. Examples include riding the school bus alone, entering the school building without your help, speaking to other kids at school, giving an oral presentation, and performing at a concert. These are significant accomplishments, so praise your child for them! In addition, praise your child for continuing to do difficult things like going to school now.

Continue to ignore minor complaints about having to attend school. Your child will likely "test" you later on by complaining about school, crying about being away from you, or feeling unwell. Continue to be supportive, but do not give these behaviors and statements too much attention. Again, let your rewards, punishments, and contracts do your talking for you. And do not worry too much if your child does start complaining again about school. Some parents think, "Here we go again!" and assume they are back to square one. But this is not the case. Your child is likely seeing what kind of reaction he can get from you. If your child sees that he is not going to get away with anything, that he has to go to school and that you are not falling into this trap, then his complaints will taper off.

Expect your child to attend school every day. This is more an attitude than anything else, but the idea is that you should expect attendance rather than absence from school. *Every day!* Adopting this attitude frees you from worry about what will happen in the morning because *only extraordinary events* (horrible weather, severe illness) should keep your child home from school. Make every effort to get your child to school even when he feels "a little under the weather" or when you have trouble one day getting him to school. Remember that it is far better for your child to go to school for 4 out of 6 hours than to miss school altogether that day. Always push for at least some school attendance on any given day if possible.

Finally, no backsliding! Once your child has shown that he can attend school and classes regularly, this is the *minimum behavior* you should expect. Do not allow your child to wiggle out of having to go to school and do not allow him any breathing room for missing school. If your child does skip school, then find him and punish the behavior. If he goes to school regularly, then be sure to reward the behavior.

Special Circumstances Regarding Your Family or Your Child

I fully appreciate that your family or your child may have special circumstances that may limit the usefulness of the methods discussed in this book. Let's talk about those circumstances that I have run into most over the years. One special circumstance is that you may have to leave for work before your child has to go to school. In this situation, try to have another adult stay with your child and be sure that he makes it to school. If no one is available, then call a taxi or arrange some supervised ride for your child to get to school. Be sure to check that he actually went to school and what went wrong if he did not. If the school attendance problem continues and you have no one else to take your child to school, then you may need to make special work arrangements so that you can go in later after you take your child to school. I know this situation can be very hard to deal with, but your child's school attendance must be a top priority.

Another special circumstance involves multiple children in a family who are refusing to go to school. You may have two or three children of different ages who will not go to school. Or you may have one child who is refusing to go to school and another child is starting to copy behaviors such as dawdling or throwing tantrums. If your children are refusing to go to school for the same reason, such as to get attention from you, then you can use the methods described in this book for each child (see chapter 5). If your children are refusing to go to school for different reasons, then you could use different methods for each child (such as chapter 3 for one child and chapter 5 for another child). Or you could use both methods for both children. For example, both children could practice relaxation exercises (see chapter 3) and both could be on a set morning schedule with rewards and punishments (see chapter 5).

Another option is to spend most of your time working with the child who is missing the most school or has the most difficult school refusal behavior. Often this child is the oldest of the children who are refusing to go to school. In this case, use the methods in this book and concentrate most on this child. As the other children see what is happening, which we hope involves more school attendance, they are more likely to fall in line and go to school themselves. Even if this is not the case, though, having your most difficult child go to school frees up your time to concentrate on the other kids. Finally, and most importantly in this situation, *get help!* Find other people who can help you complete the morning routine and who can take your kids to school.

Another special circumstance involves children with developmental disorders who refuse to go to school. This may include a child with a learning disorder who is frustrated about his schoolwork, but may also include children with more severe developmental disorders such as autism or mental retardation. In all of these cases, work closely with school officials to design a 504 or individualized education plan that includes methods for improving school attendance, such as the ones described in this book. This is especially important for designing part-time attendance schedules. In addition, meet with school officials often to see what problems at school might be resolved. If a child with a reading disorder feels unmotivated, for example, then some reward-based program at school might be helpful.

Another special circumstance involves families who have been referred to the legal/court system because of their child's absenteeism. For example, school officials will sometimes refer a family to the legal/court system for educational neglect (or other related statute) should a child miss a lot of school. If this has happened, then get as much information as you can about what is going to happen next. Do you need a lawyer? Do you have to meet with a juvenile detention officer? Do you have to go to "truancy" court? Will your child be removed from your home?

Every state is different, so I cannot give you detailed recommendations about what will happen. However, my general recommendation is to work closely with school and legal officials to resolve your child's school refusal behavior as soon as possible. Show that you are motivated to help solve this problem by attending meetings and doing what you can to get your child in school for at least part of the day. In my experience, school and legal officials are generally much more interested in getting a child back to school than in pursuing formal charges.

What to Do If You Have Not Found the Methods in This Book to Be Very Helpful

I hope you did find the methods in this book to be helpful, but what if problems seem to be lingering? Some parents say, for example, that their child now goes to school for part of the day but can't quite seem to go a full day. Other parents say their child now goes to school but still seems upset. Still other parents say that nothing seems to have worked. What now?

A couple of things might be happening. First, perhaps the methods in this book have not yet been tried long enough. I know it takes a lot of patience and persistence, but school refusal behavior problems sometimes need to be worked on for at least a few weeks before significant results are seen. In addition, the longer a child has been having problems going to school, the longer it usually takes for him to go back to school. If a school attendance problem has been developing for some time, it will take some time to fix. So, if you have been using the methods for only a couple of weeks, I encourage you to keep going. Also, meet with school officials to set up a timeline for these methods. For example, you and they may agree to try certain methods for 3 weeks and then evaluate whether they are working.

If not, then the methods could be "tweaked" a bit or some new strategy could be tried.

Second, perhaps the methods in this book are not being used consistently. This is the most likely problem. Because a child's school refusal behavior is so unpredictable, parents sometimes fall into the trap of using the methods in this book on "bad" days and not on "good" days. Many parents wait and see what kind of behavior they are going to get from their child in the morning and then *respond* to the behavior ("dancing to the child's tune;" see chapter 5). For example, a child may dawdle one morning, so parents use the structured morning routine. On another day, however, he may get ready for school with little problem, so the structured morning routine is pushed aside.

Being inconsistent holds several dangers. One danger is that you are constantly responding to your child's behavior instead of the other way around. Your child must respond to *your* expectations, rules, rewards, punishments, and meetings. If you consistently use a set morning routine or a contract, for example, then your child is always responding to what *you* set up and not the other way around. Another danger of being inconsistent is that children will not take seriously the methods described in this book. They are looking to you as the role model, so if you do not take the methods seriously, they will not either. Finally, being inconsistent allows children to think they might be able to exploit their parents and miss school. Children are more willing to test their parents if they know there is a chance the parents will "give in" and allow them to miss school.

Third, perhaps some other problem is going on that is preventing the methods in this book from being fully effective. Something unusual may have happened while you were trying to get your child to go back to school. Examples of unusual events include the birth of a new baby, an illness in the family, a car accident, job loss, a sudden move to a new area, or some other special event that may have caused distress. If this is the case, think about whether you are truly ready to put forth the effort needed to get your child back in school with less distress. If you feel you can, then see how you can "work around" major events to still accomplish what you want to accomplish. If Mom is in the hospital, for example, can other people help bring a child to school?

If you do not feel truly able to put forth the effort needed to get your child back in school at this time, then work closely with school officials to let them know what is happening. In addition, schedule an extended timeline for getting your child back to school or seek some "stopgap" measure such as home schooling or another alternative school setting so your child is receiving an education while you are dealing with whatever stressor has arisen. Try not to delay your child's education if possible.

Fourth, this book may not be completely right for your situation. In chapter 1 and in other chapters, I outlined different situations that might make this book less helpful. Examples include school refusal behavior for a long period of time, severe behavior problems in addition to school refusal behavior, and intense fighting among family members. If you find that you cannot use the methods in this book because one or more of these situations is interfering, then you may wish to consult a qualified mental health professional (see chapter 1). A qualified mental health professional can help you address severe problems that are happening within your child or family. In many cases, school refusal behavior is simply one part of these severe problems. A qualified mental health professional can help you deal with all of these problems at once because he or she will know the unique issues that you are facing.

More Technical Information About the Methods Described in This Book

All of the methods described in this book are based on scientific research and my extensive experience working with kids with school refusal behavior. Although it is not necessary to read the technical information behind the methods covered in this book, some people like to read additional material to find out more about the nature, cause, assessment, and treatment of school refusal behavior in children. I have included a "Readings and Additional Resources" section at the back of this book where you can find a listing of books, book chapters, and journal articles that contain further information on school refusal behavior.

▮ *Final Comments*

Thank you for reading this book! I appreciate the fact that you are willing to make the effort to get your child back to school with less distress. I hope you find my recommendations helpful now and in the future. If you find that your child's school refusal behavior has some special circumstance that I did not cover in this book, please let me know. Most of all, remember that you are not alone. Many parents face what you are facing, and many professionals study this problem. Together we can make a difference!

Readings and Additional Resources

Kearney, C. A. (2001). *School refusal behavior in youth: A functional approach to assessment and treatment*. Washington, DC: American Psychological Association.

Kearney, C. A. (2002). Case study of the assessment and treatment of a youth with multifunction school refusal behavior. *Clinical Case Studies, 1*, 67–80.

Kearney, C. A. (2002). Identifying the function of school refusal behavior: A revision of the School Refusal Assessment Scale. *Journal of Psychopathology and Behavioral Assessment, 24*, 235–245.

Kearney, C. A. (2003). Bridging the gap among professionals who address youth with school absenteeism: Overview and suggestions for consensus. *Professional Psychology: Research and Practice, 34*, 57–65.

Kearney, C. A. (2004). Absenteeism. In T. S. Watson & C. H. Skinner (Eds.), *Encyclopedia of school psychology* (pp. 1–2). New York: Kluwer Academic/Plenum.

Kearney, C. A. (2004). School refusal. In T. S. Watson & C. H. Skinner (Eds.), *Encyclopedia of school psychology* (pp. 274–276). New York: Kluwer Academic/Plenum.

Kearney, C. A. (2004). School refusal behavior. In W. E. Craighead & C. B. Nemeroff (Eds.), *The concise Corsini encyclopedia of psychology and behavioral science* (3rd ed.) (pp. 851–852). New York: Wiley.

Kearney, C. A. (2006). Confirmatory factor analysis of the School Refusal Assessment Scale—Revised: Child and parent versions. *Journal of Psychopathology and Behavioral Assessment, 28*, 139–144.

Kearney, C. A., & Albano, A. M. (2004). The functional profiles of school refusal behavior: Diagnostic aspects. *Behavior Modification, 28*, 147–161.

Kearney, C. A., & Albano, A. M. (2007). *When children refuse school: A cognitive-behavioral therapy approach/Parent workbook* (2nd ed.). New York: Oxford University Press.

Kearney, C. A., & Albano, A. M. (2007). *When children refuse school: A cognitive-behavioral therapy approach/Therapist's guide* (2nd ed.). New York: Oxford University Press.

Kearney, C. A., & Alvarez, K. M. (2004). Manualized treatment for school-refusal behavior in youth. In L. L'Abate (Ed.), *Using workbooks in mental health: Resources in prevention, psychotherapy, and rehabilitation for clinicians and researchers* (pp. 283–299). New York: Haworth.

Kearney, C. A., & Bates, M. (2005). Addressing school refusal behavior: Suggestions for frontline professionals. *Children and Schools, 27,* 207–216.

Kearney, C. A., & Bensaheb, A. (2006). School absenteeism and school refusal behavior: A review and suggestions for school-based health professionals. *Journal of School Health, 76,* 1–5.

Kearney, C. A., Chapman, G., & Cook, L. C. (2005). Moving from assessment to treatment of school refusal behavior in youth. *International Journal of Behavioral and Consultation Therapy, 1,* 46–51.

Kearney, C. A., Chapman, G., & Cook, L. C. (2005). School refusal behavior in young children. *International Journal of Behavioral and Consultation Therapy, 1,* 212–218.

Kearney, C. A., & Hugelshofer, D. (2000). Systemic and clinical strategies for preventing school refusal behavior in youth. *Journal of Cognitive Psychotherapy, 14,* 51–65.

Kearney, C.A., Lemos, A., & Silverman, J. (2004). The functional assessment of school refusal behavior. *Behavior Analyst Today, 5,* 275–283.

Kearney, C. A., Lemos, A., & Silverman, J. (2006). School refusal behavior. In R. B. Mennuti, A. Freeman, & R. W. Christner (Eds.), *Cognitive-behavioral interventions in educational settings: A handbook for practice* (pp. 89–105). New York: Brunner-Routledge.

Kearney, C. A., & Mizrachi, R. (1998). Interventions with school refusal behavior. In D. A. Sabatino & B. L. Brooks (Eds.), *Contemporary interdisciplinary interventions for children with emotional/behavioral disorders* (pp. 247–265). Durham, NC: Carolina Academic Press.

Kearney, C. A., & Pursell, C. (2000). School stress and school refusal behavior. In G. Fink (Ed.), *Encyclopedia of stress* (Vol. 3) (pp. 398–402). San Diego, CA: Academic Press.

Kearney, C. A., Pursell, C., & Alvarez, K. (2001). Treatment of school refusal behavior in children with mixed functional profiles. *Cognitive and Behavioral Practice, 8,* 3–11.

Kearney, C. A., & Roblek, T. L. (1998). Parent training in the treatment of school refusal behavior. In J. M. Briesmeister & C. E. Schaefer (Eds.), *Handbook of parent training: Parents as co-therapists for children's behavior problems* (2nd ed.) (pp. 225–256). New York: Wiley.

Kearney, C. A., & Silverman, W. K. (1996). The evolution and reconciliation of taxonomic strategies for school refusal behavior. *Clinical Psychology: Science and Practice, 3,* 339–354.

Kearney, C. A., & Silverman, W. K. (1999). Functionally-based prescriptive and nonprescriptive treatment for children and adolescents with school refusal behavior. *Behavior Therapy, 30,* 673–695.

Kearney, C. A., & Sims, K. E. (1997). A clinical perspective on school refusal in youngsters. *In Session: Psychotherapy in Practice, 3,* 5–19.

Kearney, C. A., Sims, K. E., Pursell, C. R., & Tillotson, C. A. (2003). Separation anxiety disorder in young children: A longitudinal and family analysis. *Journal of Clinical Child and Adolescent Psychology, 32,* 593–598.

Kearney, C. A., & Tillotson, C. A. (1998). School attendance. In T. S. Watson & F. M. Gresham (Eds.), *Handbook of child behavior therapy* (pp. 143–161). New York: Plenum.

Kearney, C. A., & Tillotson, C. A. (1998). The School Refusal Assessment Scale. In C. P. Zalaquett & R. J. Wood (Eds.), *Evaluating stress: A book of resources* (Vol. 2) (pp. 239–258). Lanham, MD: Scarecrow Press.

Below is a list of other references regarding or related to school refusal behavior. These references are more relevant to youths who refuse school because of some distress. These youths were discussed at length in chapters 3 and 4 and to some extent in chapter 5:

Beidel, D. C., & Turner, S. M. (2005). *Childhood anxiety disorders: A guide to research and treatment.* New York: Routledge.

Eisen, A. R., & Schaefer, C. E. (2005). *Separation anxiety in children and adolescents: An individualized approach to assessment and treatment.* New York: Guilford.

Heyne, D., & Rollings, S. (2002). *School refusal.* Malden, MA: Blackwell.

Kearney, C.A. (2005). *Social anxiety and social phobia in youth: Characteristics, assessment, and psychological treatment.* New York: Springer.

Morris, T. L., & March, J. S. (2004). *Anxiety disorders in children and adolescents* (2nd ed.). New York: Guilford.

Ollendick, T. H., & Cerny, J. A. (1981). *Clinical behavior therapy with children.* New York: Plenum (now Springer).

Ollendick, T. H., & March, J. S. (2004). *Phobic and anxiety disorders in children and adolescents: A clinician's guide to effective psychosocial and pharmacological interventions.* New York: Oxford University Press.

Silverman, W. K., & Kurtines, W. M. (1996). *Anxiety and phobic disorders: A pragmatic approach.* New York: Plenum (now Springer).

Silverman, W. K., & Treffers, P. D. A. (2001). *Anxiety disorders in children and adolescents: Research, assessment and intervention.* New York: Cambridge University Press.

CPSIA information can be obtained
at www.ICGtesting.com
Printed in the USA
BVHW050453120819
555615BV00003B/10/P